DATE DUE

MAR 07 2005	
GAYLORD	PRINTED IN U.S.A.

Josiah Walls

Josiah Walls
1842-1905

Josiah Walls

Florida's Black Congressman
of Reconstruction

Peter D. Klingman

A University of Florida Book

The University Presses of Florida
Gainesville / 1976

Library of Congress Cataloging in Publication Data

Klingman, Peter D.   1945–
  Josiah Walls: Florida's Black Congressman of
Reconstruction.

  "A University of Florida book."
  Bibliography: p.
  Includes index.
  1. Walls, Josiah T., 1842–1905. 2. Negroes—
History—1863–1877. 3. Negroes—Politics and suffrage.
E664.W19K54   975.9'06'0924 [B]   75–45206
ISBN 0–8130–0399–7

TYPOGRAPHY BY CANON GRAPHICS
TALLAHASSEE, FLORIDA

PRINTED BY THE STORTER PRINTING COMPANY, INCORPORATED
GAINESVILLE, FLORIDA

Acknowledgments

MANY people deserve my sincere thanks for their help with this project, but I especially wish to thank Dr. Samuel Proctor, professor and friend, for his many suggestions, comments, and keen criticism. He saved this manuscript from countless errors in style, organization, and content. Whatever errors remain are, of course, mine alone.

For their assistance in research, I would like to thank the staffs of the following libraries and repositories: the P. K. Yonge Library of Florida History and Miss Elizabeth A. Alexander; the University of Florida Research Library and Mr. Ray Jones; the Amisted Research Center and Mr. Clifton Johnson; the National Archives and Mr. James Walker; the Library of Congress; and the Southern Historical Collection, University of North Carolina at Chapel Hill.

A special debt is owed to Professor William C. Childers, Department of English, University of Florida, for kindly allowing me to examine and cite from the Garth James Papers in his possession, and to Professor Jerrell H. Shofner, chairman of the Department of History, Florida Technological University, for directing me to sources as well as for his insight into Florida's Reconstruction. Last, I should like to thank my wife, Nina, for she really understands how it feels to share one's life with a man named Walls.

Preface

ANDRÉ GIDE once remarked that greater wisdom lay in asking how, rather than why, events happen. By examining the public career of one man, I hope that this study will shed light on that question as it concerns Josiah Walls and black political participation during Florida's Reconstruction. Although there were other black politicians in the state during that period—John Wallace, Henry Harmon, Charles Pearce, and Robert Meacham, for example—none attained the stature or received the attention given Walls throughout his career. Unfortunately, however, he has eluded history as a man; only his public image remains, and that is incomplete. In consequence, answers to the basic questions of how he managed his life are difficult to ascertain. Little remains to provide us with his views. No one can accurately state what things affected him, or how, or what forces shaped his life.

What has survived about Josiah Walls consists for the most part of newspaper references to his many political campaigns and elections, the documentary evidence of his two contested election cases heard before the Congress, the journals of the House of Representatives and of the Florida legislature outlining his role as a member of each, and a few descriptions left by contemporaries. Only a letter or two in Walls' own hand have survived. He and his widow filed for pensions from the federal government, and these applications comprise major sources of biographical data, including descriptions of Walls' health, his second marriage license, and other materials. In 1971, moreover, this author interviewed two elderly residents in Tallahassee who knew Josiah Walls and his family during his last years following his move there from Alachua County, near the turn of the century.

With this limited material it has been possible to reconstruct the public life of Josiah Walls. It is not a complete biography. I hope it is at least a satisfactory attempt to focus upon the major Negro politician of Reconstruction Florida and, in so doing, to gain new insight into black political participation during that era.

But if this is to be more than sheer narrative, the reader also must recognize its interpretive framework. In this study I examine Walls not by measuring what he accomplished or failed to accomplish for his race, but by focusing on how he functioned in an era of racial conservatism in Republican policies and politics. Because of that racially determined fact, the traditional tests for politicians, such as power or prestige, success or influence, fail when applied to Walls or, indeed, to any of the Reconstruction Negro officeholders. Apart from all questions as to his native ability, Josiah Walls lacked the basic strength to bring about significant changes for his race.

Yet, within definite limits, Walls not only survived but succeeded in an age when neither survival nor success was guaranteed to a Negro. There cannot, however, be an in-depth probe into the reasons. What there can be is a look at a man and his participation in Reconstruction politics on the local, state, and national levels. And if Gide was right, then in this pursuit the reader perhaps may capture some of the flavor of the kind of man Josiah Walls was.

Research into Josiah Walls' public career produced a variety of problems in assembling information. As indicated, he did not leave a collection of papers or records for analysis, thereby negating any concerted effort at "fleshing out" his personality. There are at least three reasons for this absence of personal materials. First is the possibility of Walls' own lack of a sense of history and the importance of his role therein. Second, he may have been indifferent to recordkeeping. Then, too, the carelessness of record preservation in the nineteenth century probably has led to the destruction of much correspondence of that time; records were simply not kept in the systematic fashion of today. This lack was undoubtedly compounded by the fact that Walls was black. Apart from Frederick Douglass, few black leaders in the period engaged in lengthy correspondence with white contemporaries; as a result, their messages and letters for the most part were not saved, and those few which have reached the present arrived more as a matter of chance than a matter of course. With the advent of the emphasis upon balancing the record of the

American past through incorporation of the black experience, this lack has been sorely felt. The result has been a plethora of works on Negro history, encompassing primarily the relations of whites to blacks. The few black biographies are of major figures only—Frederick Douglass, Booker T. Washington, or W. E. B. DuBois, for example. Men like Walls have been ignored. This study, then, represents an attempt to correct the balance. It is a look at a black man who, despite relative anonymity, wielded influence among his people.

The impetus for this project came from my previous examination of the Negro Convention Movement in Reconstruction. In assessing the attitudes of the black national leadership toward the Republican party, I discovered that not only did Josiah Walls play an important role in two of the largest conventions of the period, but he also took a rather dim view of the party early in Reconstruction. I became interested in this black man who would choose to nominate another of his race as a candidate for the vice presidency of the United States in a South Carolina convention at the same time the state was put under martial law because of the Ku Klux Klan.[1]

It was then I discovered that secondary references and treatments of Walls had been limited in scope and interpretation. The absence of materials had most likely been the primary cause, although a thorough search had not yet been undertaken. Samuel Denny Smith, following the racially biased framework popularized by William A. Dunning, outlined Walls' career in the House of Representatives. In Smith's view, Walls and also the other black congressmen of Reconstruction were, for the most part, uneducated and ill prepared for the responsibilities of national elective office. He concluded they were inconsequential in influence and narrowly concerned with racial affairs.[2] In a more recent study of the Negro in Reconstruction Florida, Joe M. Richardson presented a more sympathetic view of Walls.[3] Unfortunately, he relied heavily upon the period's major historian, Dunningite scholar William Watson Davis, as well as Smith's early work and John Wallace's contemporary account of the period (discredited because of its bias and / or the direct influence of William D. Bloxham).[4] Handicapped by a lack of

1. Peter D. Klingman, "The National Negro Convention Movement, 1864–1872: Black Leadership Attitudes toward the Republican Party," passim. Complete citations may be found in the Bibliography.
2. *The Negro in Congress, 1870–1901*, pp. 74–78.
3. *The Negro in the Reconstruction of Florida, 1865–1877*, pp. 177–83.
4. *Carpetbag Rule in Florida*, p. xxiv. It is believed by some that Governor Bloxham

sources, Richardson did an injustice to Walls by a superficial treatment based on heavily biased secondary studies. None of the other few references to Walls in theses, dissertations, and articles on Florida's Reconstruction have examined in depth his role in the events of the era. Thus, it is hoped that this study will fill a void in the scholarly body of knowledge about an important man in one of the important periods in American history.

A word needs to be said also about terminology. The reader will note that "Negro" is used in the text, and that "colored," when part of a direct quotation, has not been deleted. These were common terms utilized in this period by both races. As this is not a study of or a reflection upon current moods, no attempt has been made to distort the account by an artificial use of "Black" or "Afro-American."

---

actually wrote the entire account and had it published under the authorship of Wallace, a freedman who taught school on Bloxham's plantation in the first days of emancipation.

Contents

To Nina and Abby

1

Out of the Conflict

Washington, D.C., had changed a great deal by the spring of 1874. The Civil War lay almost a decade behind, although its marks and scars were still quite visible. Union troops remained stationed in parts of the South, and it did not seem to matter to most white Southerners that their numbers were scanty. Republicans no longer controlled the federal government, for the Democratic party had made large gains in the fall elections. Charles Sumner, the high priest of radicalism, died in March, and with his passing went many Negroes' hopes and dreams of equality. The economic panic of 1873 also contributed to the new outlook. It affected all citizens—white and black—and, in its wake, purely political concerns gave way to other issues, such as greenbacks or silver and the prices for foodstuffs. Tariffs and taxes were discussed more frequently than the activities of scalawags and carpetbaggers; western agrarians and eastern capitalists overshadowed the unionist-rebel controversy. And although Cuba and Santo Domingo remained important topics in foreign affairs, there was no real threat of war in 1874, especially since England had settled the *Alabama* claims two years earlier.

On May 8, 1874, a young man stood on the floor of the House of Representatives to address his fellow congressmen. He was only thirty-one, tall and slender, with short, curly, brown hair. His dark brown eyes cast off a serious gaze, and those who looked at him while he spoke noticed the straight nose and full moustache covering his upper lip. His speech suggested that he had worked hard in its preparation, researching his facts and practicing his delivery. He was not an accomplished orator, having a tendency to read his speeches too closely, but he was a serious and intense man trying to do his best under difficult conditions.

1

His topic that spring day was the matter of a $3-million appropriation for the Philadelphia Exposition that would mark the centennial celebration of American independence in 1876. Some representatives thought the matter unimportant and others objected to the size of the proposed grant. The young congressman preferred to stress its advantages. He emphasized its unifying potential and concluded that, above all else, "when from every corner of this broad land . . . free citizens of a free government shall assemble in the very cradle and the place of birth of all . . . they hold dear, and exchange with each other the mutual grasp and the meaningful glances of common citizenship . . . all questions of differences and all hurtful recollections will be blotted out."

It is true, of course, that in the very hall in which this man, Josiah T. Walls, congressman from the second electoral district in Florida, was speaking, many such patriotic and stirring words had been uttered before, about America, its people, and their common bonds. But more recently there had been only passionate and angry debate about two "countries," North and South, a divided people, and slavery. Out of the ensuing conflict many changes had occurred, one of the most important of which was the death of slavery. Without emancipation Josiah Walls would never have been standing there, in the seat of national government, addressing Congress on any subject: he was a black man and, in all likelihood, a former slave from the hills of northwestern Virginia. Without emancipation, he would not have been elected to the House of Representatives on three separate occasions, nor elected to one term in the Florida state assembly and two in the state senate. It would have been impossible for him to have been appointed a brigadier general in the Florida state militia with black and white troops under his command. Without emancipation, he could not have become mayor, county commissioner, newspaper publisher and editor, attorney, or successful landowner and farmer—particularly not in the South. Josiah Walls achieved all these public and private positions during the period from 1868 to 1884.

There are some preliminary factors to consider about Florida after the war that can help the reader. Florida emerged from the Civil War remarkably untouched by the kinds and the degrees of devastation witnessed in other Confederate states. The state never experienced a Shermanesque march across its interior or a bloodbath such as Grant washed over Virginia in the last weeks before Appomattox. At war's end, Florida was still a frontier state, sparsely settled and remote.

This isolation worked its way into Florida's Reconstruction. To a degree not felt elsewhere in the South, Florida's Republican party tore itself apart through intense factionalism. The intra-Republican divisions, evident from the outset of military Reconstruction, rested on much more than the traditional carpetbag-scalawag-freedmen tripod. The freedmen themselves were divided into two groups, one organized by the head of the Freedmen's Bureau, Thomas Osborn, and the other under the aegis of the national Republican committee. Josiah Walls was in this latter group, the mule team faction organized by Daniel Richards, Liberty Billings, and William Saunders, two whites and a Negro carpetbagger, respectively.

As was true in other states, Republicans and conservatives were also divided geographically. There were concentrations of unionists, conservatives, and freedmen. The center for Florida's native white unionists was in East Florida, primarily in Jacksonville and the surrounding area. From there, stretching westward across the northern portion of the state, were the black-belt counties, inhabited by ex-slaves and ex-slaveowners alike. In the south, especially in the central part of the peninsula, few people lived, although there were settled areas along either coast and at Key West. Nevertheless, the basic political division in Florida during this period was east and west. Even after the state was apportioned into two electoral districts following the 1870 census, and there were district conventions and executive committees in each, factional disputes in statewide politics still centered on geographical lines.

Another critical factor that must be considered was the freedman himself. In many respects the Negro population in Florida was the chief reality of Reconstruction. Unlike the more numerous free Negroes and mulattoes of Louisiana, for example, who had quite different relations with whites in the prewar era, the Florida freedmen were less able to assert themselves against whites, Republicans or Democrats. Florida also lacked Negro leaders truly capable both of working with the whites and of resisting white manipulation at the same time. Except for Jonathan Gibbs, who died too early to have a major impact, Florida had no true counterpart to South Carolina's Robert Brown Elliott, Virginia's John Mercer Langston, or Louisiana's Pinckney B. S. Pinchback—men recognized by both races to be competent, educated, and experienced.

The extent of cooperation between Josiah Walls and the other Negro leaders of Florida cannot be estimated. Jonathan Gibbs, a graduate of Dartmouth who became Florida's secretary of state under Governor Harrison Reed, died before Walls' career reached its peak. The two were in touch: Walls appointed Gibbs' son Thomas to West Point, and Gibbs testified in one of Walls' contested election cases. Beyond that, their precise relationship is unknown. One can surmise that all the Negro leaders in the state worked together whenever and wherever they could for racial improvement, but the degree of unified leadership among Negroes cannot be measured.

Unfortunately, the reader must also grapple with a difficult political word, "rings," popularized by the early histories of Florida's Reconstruction. Because of the factionalism that prevailed in Reconstruction politics, many historians have concluded that all political activity was motivated by "rings" of self-serving politicos inured to the needs of the people.[1] Two facts, at least, are clear: there were very loose ties among the various factions, and there were continual changes in alignments. Whether all politics during Florida's Reconstruction was manipulated by "rings" is, however, questionable.

The most critical aspect of the use of the word revolved around party politics and patronage. Although local issues tended to dominate local politics, and state issues dominated statewide politics, attempts were made to wrest federal or national patronage from Florida's national representatives. As a result, groups of federal officeholders were often opposed by groups of state politicians who also wanted to influence Republican patronage.

Other facets of Reconstruction politics in Florida further accentuated the concept of "rings." Because of wide citizen interest in political affairs, newspapers emphasized politics, and the partisanship of the editor counted more heavily than did standards of credibility or objectivity. Two newspapers in the same locale and nominally of the same party leaning could and did disagree over political issues, actions, and candidates. This was exacerbated when a politician edited his own newspaper, thereby creating a forum for his personal views. When two politicians who differed in this way owned and edited newspapers in the same community, as did Josiah Walls and Leonard Dennis in Gainesville in 1873, the idea of "rings" was naturally reinforced.

However, there is a special burden attached to the easy use of the word "ring" as it applied to the black vote. Walls had overwhelming Negro

1. William Watson Davis, *The Civil War and Reconstruction in Florida*, popularized this image of the Republican politican. Davis was a member of the William A. Dunning seminar at Columbia University that produced the historiographic interpretation carrying his name. It was characteristic for the Dunningite scholars to add the closely aligned image of greedy and corrupt Republicans "ravaging" the South.

support in his district throughout his career. This was necessary and inevitable, given the racial attitudes of the day. Yet there are two other factors to consider. First, not all black people were united behind Walls or any other candidate, party, or program. There were avowed Negro conservatives during the early years of Reconstruction and, later, many Negroes joined the Democratic party and other parties. It is unlikely that all were pressured by terrorism or intimidation to do so, for black leaders competed among themselves for political power and prestige. Second, and of great import, black leaders were forced to consider interests other than race. Walls and his Negro colleagues sought to avoid complete dependence upon a single group. Had they not tried this, it is inconceivable that they would have achieved even the limited success they did. After all, most freedmen would not vote against any regular Republican. Thus, one must be careful in considering why Walls decided to engage himself politically in the manner he did. It was a complex political arena, and no one, black or white, had the key to its total control.

2

Soldier to State Senator

SOMEWHERE among the rolling hills north of the Shenandoah Valley in northwestern Virginia, Josiah T. Walls was born on December 30, 1842. Nothing is known of the circumstances of his birth except that it was in or near Winchester in Frederick County. No clues remain concerning the identity of his parents, the size of his family, or even if he was born slave or free. Walls at one time stated that his parents were free by 1842; however, on another occasion he remarked that he never felt "the daylight of freedom" until he had enlisted in the Union army in 1863.[1] Most of the evidence indicates that Walls was born in slavery. His military records labeled him as "free after 1863," a common notation in the files of black soldiers who had escaped slavery and enlisted in the Union cause. A contemporary of his in Florida later described Walls' journeys, while a member of Congress, into Virginia "to see his former master and mistress," whom he "always spoke of . . . in the kindest terms."[2] Moreover, if Walls in fact was impressed into Confederate service and captured at the Battle of Yorktown, as has been claimed,[3] it is even more likely that his impressment was as a slave; there would have been less reason to carry a free black northward. Available census data and the Frederick County courthouse records shed no light on Walls' background or early life.

The Winchester region attracted both slaveholders and nonslave-

1. *Tallahassee Sentinel*, August 27, 1870, September 28, 1872.
2. James H. Roper to E. C. F. Sanchez, n.d., E. C. F. Sanchez Papers.
3. William H. Barnes, *Our American Government: History of the Forty-Third Congress*, 3:216–17.

holders to its fertile lands and strategic location. Lying across the northern entrance to the Shenandoah Valley, Winchester, the present-day county seat of Frederick County, was laid out in 1744. Enlarged and renamed in 1752, it developed into an agricultural entrepôt for the transfer of foodstuffs to and from the eastern seaboard. Thus, the area attracted both kinds of settlers from the stream of pioneers who pushed westward in search of prosperous land.[4] During the early years of his life Walls moved from Winchester to Darkesville, located in Berkeley County, then still in Virginia.[5] Then as now, Darkesville was a small rural community composed of approximately equal numbers of whites and blacks. The village was named for William Darke, Revolutionary War general, but had been established originally under a 1791 land grant to James Buckells, the largest landowner in the region at that time. Situated on the Winchester-Martinsburg turnpike at the junction of Middle Creek, the town's population had reached only 195 by 1840.[6] Again, the circumstances of this aspect of Walls' boyhood are unknown, as are the facts concerning his education. The speeches of his later career indicate that Walls was an educated man; however, his only known schooling took place in Harrisburg, Pennsylvania, paid for by a "private source," and achieved "by his own application and industry."[7] The exact dates and details are unclear and puzzling. If he did serve for a brief time in the service of the Confederacy until 1862, and enlisted in the Union army in mid-1863, his formal education must have been limited. It is likely that any schooling he did receive was at the county normal school, as it was one of only two schools operating in Harrisburg at that time; the other was an academy.[8] Yet, possessed of a strong, legible handwriting and mature vocabulary, Walls managed to gain more than just the rudiments of an education.

He enlisted as a private in the Third Infantry Regiment, United States Colored Troops, in July 1863. He was mustered in for three years on July 9 at Philadelphia. His regiment was the first of eleven black units

---

4. Frederick Morton, *The Story of Winchester in Virginia: The Oldest Town in the Shenandoah Valley*, p. 147.

5. *Tallahassee Sentinel*, September 10, 1870. Darkesville is approximately 14 miles north of Winchester on U.S. 11 in present-day West Virginia.

6. Mabel H. Gardiner and Ann H. Gardiner, *Chronicles of Old Berkeley: A Narrative History of a Virginia County from Its Beginnings to 1926*, pp. 47–48. The 1840 census for Darkesville was prepared by J. Q. Nadenbousch, the assistant marshal of Berkeley County. (Martinsburg) *Virginia Free Press*, December 3, 1840.

7. Roper to Sanchez, n.d., Sanchez Papers.

8. *Report of the Superintendent of Common Schools of Pennsylvania, 1862*. There are no extant records for either school at the time of Walls' attendance.

raised in Pennsylvania by the Philadelphia Supervisory Committee for
Recruiting Colored Soldiers and was commanded by Col. Benjamin
Tilghman, breveted in 1865 as a brigadier general in Tallahassee.[9] Walls'
military service included almost the entire agenda of the regiment's
movements, from its inception to its disbandment in Florida in 1865.

After it had been organized, the unit underwent a brief and inadequate
basic training period at Camp William Penn, outside Philadelphia. From
here the Third was ordered attached to the Department of the South and
was assigned to Morris Island, South Carolina, where it remained
through 1864.[10] With the exception of the siege and assaults on Forts
Wagner and Gregg during August and September 1863, the unit suffered through a long period of inactivity broken only by the tediousness
of guard duty. Having had only a few days of basic training, the
regiment lacked proper military organization.

According to Colonel Tilghman this deficiency was a result of discrimination against black troops. In a letter to the assistant adjutant
general of the Department of the South, Tilghman complained of his
regiment's treatment in South Carolina: "The Reg't was sent to this
Dept. within a few days of its enlistment. Since arriving here, it has been
exclusively employed on siege or fatigue duty, consequently the men are
as to drill and instruction, raw recruits. In target practice, skirmishing
and battalion movements they are utterly uninstructed. By an order in
force at this post the white conscripts recently arrived are excluded from
fatigue duty, and all their time is devoted to drill."[11]

He also was disturbed about the general health condition of his troops.
The medical records indicate that the proportion of sickness among black
soldiers, which according to Tilghman stood at 12.2 per cent, was 1.74
times greater than among their white counterparts. Walls himself was
afflicted at this time with a severe case of diarrhea, hemorrhoids, and an
unknown eye disease that continued to plague him for the rest of his
life.[12] One cause of the poor health among the members of Walls'
regiment was the long hours they spent in the swamps surrounding the

9. Josiah T. Walls Service File; Frederick M. Binder, "Pennsylvania Negro Regiments
in the Civil War," p. 395.

10. Frederick H. Dyer, *A Compendium of the War of the Rebellion*, 3:1723; Benjamin
Tilghman to Assistant Adjutant General, Jacksonville, June 23, 1865, in "Orders, Letters,
and Roster of Commissioned Officers, Endorsements, and Memoranda, Third Infantry
Regiment, U.S.C.T."

11. Tilghman to Adjutant General, Morris Island, South Carolina, December 1863, in
"Orders and Letters."

12. Josiah T. Walls Pension File. Walls filed for a pension in March 1892, and
described his medical problems as having attacked him "off and on" for about thirty years.

fort at Morris Island, cutting sod in the cold and wet. The "rough and dirty" work wore out shoes and clothing at a rapid pace, a hardship upon men who received no special clothing allotment. Tilghman pointed out that these conditions lowered morale and were of greater import to the men than either poor health or lack of military instruction: "They begin to believe that they are not intended for soldiers, but merely drudges to do the hard and dirty work; whereas to make them reliable troops their self respect and pride in their profession should be cultivated in every reasonable way."[13]

Ill health, fatigue duty, and improper training were not the only problems black soldiers endured by joining the war effort. The Third Regiment, along with all other black organizations, suffered from unequal pay scales. The normal $3 clothing allowance, an addition to the pay of white soldiers, was subtracted from their regular $10 per month wages. Extra issues of clothing became necessary to "keep a soldierly appearance" while engaged in siege and fatigue details.[14] In January 1864, Tilghman indignantly wrote his superiors that the extra clothing had amounted to $41 per man since the regiment had been formed, equaling 80 per cent of its pay and allowances. Nine of his men had been killed after only one month of service, but their clothing bills totaled $30 per man in that short space of time. This debt had to be assumed by their survivors before the federal government paid bounties or pensions. Moreover, black noncommissioned officers did not receive increased pay with their promotions.[15] Walls was affected by this situation, as he had been promoted to corporal in October 1863.[16]

The regiment joined the Florida campaign under the command of Gen. Truman Seymour in February 1864. By this time foodstuffs were in short supply throughout the Confederacy, a result of Union raids in the southeast and Grant's success at cutting off the farmlands west of the Mississippi. These factors, and the steady drain of available food for the armies, had created widespread discontent within the Confederacy in Florida. In an attempt to deny the Confederates the beef, bacon, and grain of middle Florida and the salt and goods slipping through the blockade from its coasts, the North decided to invade the state in early 1864.

The regiment was stationed first at Baldwin, which had been a

13. Tilghman to Assistant Adjutant General, Morris Island, in "Orders and Letters."
14. Ibid.
15. Ibid., January 17, 1864.
16. Josiah T. Walls Service File.

strategic Confederate supply depot to the west of Jacksonville. Although it did not take part in the Battle of Olustee, the Third moved back to Jacksonville after the Confederates blunted the federal drive across the state. Walls' unit was then assigned to garrison the city until the close of the war and was bivouacked east of the city. The troops participated in many of the maneuvers and raids inland that were undertaken to weaken southern resistance. One aspect of their duty was to bring into their lines as many freedmen as possible, a major reason for the use of black troops during the Florida campaign.[17] During one raid near St. Augustine in March, a twenty-five-man patrol from the Third brought in seventy slaves.[18]

Walls was transferred in June 1864, to join the Thirty-fifth United States Colored Troops stationed in Picolata, a settlement on the St. Johns River near St. Augustine. He had been promoted to first sergeant in March, and was assigned as an artillery instructor with his new regiment. He mustered out on October 31, 1865, with a debt of $6.00 to the army and a credit of $18.66 in back pay plus his service bounty of $100.00. In general, Walls' military record is not very distinguished. He received no citations, either for merit or discipline, although he was considered responsible enough to command at least one prisoner detail escorting deserters from Picolata to the provost office in Jacksonville.[19]

The officer corps of his regiment had a decided influence on Josiah Walls, not only from a military standpoint, but also after he had begun to achieve political prominence in Florida. Three officers who were to figure in his later activities were William K. Cessna, lieutenant and platoon leader in Company A, Sherman Conant, captain and commander of Company H, and Gen. William Birney, whose order to transfer Walls resulted in the reassignment to Picolata. Birney later became an editor for the Walls-owned (Gainesville) *New Era*.

Walls' own company was F, commanded by Capt. Alexander Toplanyi, who took over in August 1863 at Camp William Penn. Toplanyi remained in command for almost the entire war. The captain was not considered an able officer by his superiors: the regiment's adjutant,

17. T. Frederick Davis, *History of Jacksonville and Vicinity, 1513 to 1924*, pp. 134–35; Davis, *The Civil War and Reconstruction in Florida*, pp. 268–72; John E. Johns, *The Civil War in Florida, 1861–1865*, pp. 74–76.

18. Tilghman to Assistant Adjutant General, Jacksonville, June 23, 1865, in "Orders and Letters"; Dyer, *A Compendium of the War of the Rebellion*, 3:1723; *The War of the Rebellion: A Compilation of the Official Records of the Union and Confederate Armies*, 1st ser. 47(3):622; H. Gorham Greeley to George Whipple, March 18, 1864, American Missionary Archives, #8629.

19. Josiah T. Walls Service File.

Ulysses Doubleday, found him "incompetent, inefficient, and lacking in sense of honor."[20] Toplanyi's recordkeeping appears to have been the major reason for his poor recommendations. He was placed under arrest in Jacksonville on May 13, 1864, for neglect of his accounts and "other serious offences."[21] It was his sloppiness that created a mix-up for Walls. The regimental records and the company descriptive books did not indicate his promotion to first sergeant. Toplanyi probably failed to forward the promotion to higher headquarters. As a result, Walls was still suing the government for back pay at the higher rate even as late as 1876.[22]

The details of Walls' movements after his discharge from the army in 1865 are not clear. He married a sixteen-year-old girl, Helen Fergueson, in Newnansville on December 9, 1864.[23] She was originally from South Carolina, one of five children of Armstrong Fergueson, a farmer who lived only a short distance away from his new son-in-law. The Ferguesons were among the many immigrants, black and white, who settled in Alachua County in this period, attracted by the cheap land and its agricultural promise.[24]

Walls, like most newly married men, faced the problem of seeking a livelihood. He signed on as lumberer with the firm of Cessna and Chaires to work on the Suwannee River.[25] Cutting mill logs at that time was no simple task, as one lumberer remembered. Ambrose Hart described the logging operations on Black Creek in 1867, a picture probably similar to the life Walls lived. The lumber camps were usually situated on or near a creek that emptied into a navigable river, since there were so few roads or railroads. Log shanties were built and stocked with provisions. Mules and timber carts were employed to haul the raw lumber to the creek. The logs averaged 300 board feet when felled and were rafted together, 500 logs at a time. These huge rafts were then floated to the mills to be cut and sold. Negroes were utilized to ride the rafts down the rivers, spending most of their time in the water keeping the huge timber

20. Doubleday to Headquarters, Morris Island, November 3, 1864, in "Orders and Letters."

21. Major Bardwell to Adjutant General, Jacksonville, May 13, 1864, ibid.

22. Josiah T. Walls Service File; "Company F Descriptive Book, Third Infantry Regiment, U.S.C.T."

23. Josiah T. Walls Pension File.

24. (Gainesville) *New Era*, February 23, 1867; F. W. Buchholz, *History of Alachua County, Florida: Narrative and Biographical*, passim; Ninth U.S. Census (1870). According to order of visitation listed on the census schedule, the two families were two houses apart.

25. *Fernandina Observer*, n.d., quoted in (Jacksonville) *The New South*, August 26, 1874. The lumber firm was owned by William Cessna, an officer in Walls' regiment, and Thomas Chaires, a member of the prominent Chaires family of Tallahassee.

platforms from jamming.[26] It was hard, grueling work and also lonely, for women were not permitted in the lumber camps during the working operations. Walls did not spend much time thus engaged, however, for he soon became a school teacher in Archer.

Here, too, no details are available; yet it was quite likely that the young man landed the teaching job with little difficulty. The ex-slaves were woefully unprepared by their previous condition to assume many of the responsibilities of freedom, and education ranked as a major concern for many. Many white missionary societies as well as the Freedmen's Bureau provided teachers to inculcate the rudiments of learning to the freedmen throughout the South. Yet, there remained a continual shortage of, and thus, a continual demand for, teachers. Black teachers were desired to teach in plantation and rural schools. Academic requirements were flexible, and many of the teachers had little more knowledge than their pupils.[27] Walls, who had had at least some formal schooling, could have easily met the standards for teachers in freedmen's schools. Had not political conditions changed with the advent of military reconstruction in 1867, it is likely Walls would have continued in that capacity.

Things had changed considerably by the spring of 1867. A state Republican party emerged, although it was beset with the same divisiveness that had surfaced even before the war ended. The discord between the southern unionists and the new arrivals, who had entered Florida either with or immediately behind the federal forces, centered on the question of who would control the reorganized state government. Especially after Congress passed the Military Reconstruction Act of March 2, 1867, and more Negroes registered to vote, this issue loomed in the forefront of political discussions and plans. The Florida unionists had endured the suffering and privation of a war on their own land and, as a result, were resentful of outsiders. On the other hand, those northerners who stayed saw new opportunities for careers and influence in the fluid political situation.

The struggle quickly took on added dimensions. A federal treasury agent from Illinois, Daniel Richards, a former army officer, Liberty Billings, and a black carpetbagger from Maryland, William U. Saun-

26. Ambrose Hart to his father, January 2, 1867, Ambrose Hart Letters, mss. box 13.
27. *Fernandina Observer*, n.d., quoted in (Jacksonville) *The New South*, August 26, 1874. There is no record of Walls among the missionary society lists of Henry Swint, *The Northern Teacher in the South, 1862–1870*, appendix. For the shortage of teachers in Florida, see U.S. Bureau of Refugees, Freedmen, and Abandoned Lands, *Third Semi-Annual Report on Schools for Freedmen, January, 1867*, p. 36.

ders, began to organize the freedmen of Florida into political leagues, a mission undertaken at least in part at the behest of the national Republican party. They were competing for the control of the potential vote of the freedmen with the Freedmen's Bureau, whose entry into politics had been engineered by Bureau officer Thomas Osborn, who enrolled many Negroes in his Lincoln Brotherhoods. Even further splintering occurred in 1867 as white conservatives, disheartened at the overthrow of their political power under presidential reconstruction, proved unable to develop a single strategy. They split into active and passive groups.[28]

An awakening black interest in registration, voting, and politics poured into this already complicated milieu in the summer of 1867. This was true in Alachua County as elsewhere in Florida, and Josiah Walls soon found himself a new and rewarding career. In Alachua County, black registrants far exceeded whites, a result more of the conservative boycott than of disfranchisement. The voting for delegates to the scheduled constitutional convention in January 1868 showed 979 black votes to only 8 white votes in the November election.[29]

Mass meetings were held over the entire state in the spring and summer of 1867 as the various contenders for power attempted to consolidate their political bases. The meetings, according to John T. Sprague, head of the Bureau in Florida, "passed off in a satisfactory manner. In this city (Jacksonville) two thousand and upwards were assembled; at Gainesville quite as many; at Lake City three thousand; at Tallahassee five thousand. At these meetings speeches were made by the leading white citizens of the State and followed by intelligent colored men. A generous and mutual good feeling prevailed and the crowds dispersed in the utmost harmony."[30]

Sprague's optimistic comments were reiterated in the newspaper account of a mass meeting held in Gainesville on April 27, 1867. Although there is no proof that Walls attended, the meeting was large and both white and black people came to it. It started at the Negro church with a grand parade which wound its way to a large, open, nearby field where a platform for the speakers had been erected. An invocation was offered by

28. The following works contain accounts of the political division in Reconstruction Florida: Davis, *The Civil War and Reconstruction in Florida*; Richardson, *The Negro in the Reconstruction of Florida*; Philip D. Ackerman, "Florida Reconstruction from Walker through Reed, 1865–1873"; Jerrell H. Shofner, "Political Reconstruction in Florida"; and John A. Meador, "Florida Political Parties, 1865–1877."

29. (Gainesville) *New Era*, November 23, 1867.

30. John T. Sprague to O. O. Howard, June 5, 1867, *Letters Sent from the Assistant Commissioner of Florida*.

the Reverend Edward Deyer. The first speaker was Capt. James H. Durkee, the local Bureau agent. Durkee, who had lost an arm in the war, apparently was respected in the community, at least by the editor of the conservative Gainesville *New Era*. He was described as a man who "exercised sound discretion, acted impartially in all matters coming before him, and deserves the gratitude of all classes."[31] The agent addressed the crowd on the provisions of the military acts as they pertained to the upcoming registration of voters. Captain Durkee counseled the voters-to-be to remain trustworthy and to beware "pettifogging politicians." He was followed to the speakers' podium by Capt. E. R. Ames, the local head of the military force in the district. The meeting in general was reported to have been peaceful and a fitting testimonial to the fact that, in Alachua County, the races could successfully intermingle at public gatherings.[32] The next month a similar political rally was held in Newnansville, the small community in which the Wallses had settled after his brief teaching experience in Archer. Walls may have been one of the speakers at the rally.[33]

An early attempt on the part of the Republican party to narrow the distance between its factions came at the Republican platform convention in Tallahassee in mid-July 1867. This convention, the party's first statewide meeting, and also the first for Walls, reflected the inherent problems that eventually spelled ruin for Republican political dominance, either with or without control of the black vote. The meeting was called as a result of the efforts of Col. Ossian B. Hart, the federal registrar in East Florida, and the moderate Union-Republican Club of Jacksonville.[34]

Besides illuminating the power struggle between Republican factions, the platform convention also affords an opportunity to examine the political proscription that Negroes were to suffer in Reconstruction. Hart believed the role of the freedmen in the state's political future was one of voting, not controlling. After the summer series of mass meetings, he observed only a week prior to the Tallahassee convention that "the Freedmen are sure to go with us, if we do not let go of the hold that we have. I have attended two large mass meetings of Freedmen . . . they are strongly Republican and Radical."[35] Some historians have pointed to the

31. (Gainesville) *New Era*, May 18, 1867.

32. Ibid., May 4, 1867.

33. Ibid., May 25, 1867.

34. "Proceedings of the Union-Republican Club of Jacksonville." Hart was a native of Florida, and his father, Isaac David Hart, is sometimes called the "Father of Jacksonville."

35. *Tallahassee Semi-Weekly Floridian*, July 3, 1867.

dispute among Hart, Harrison Reed, and Thomas Osborn over the chairmanship of the convention as evidence of the internal weakness of the Republican party. They also have stressed the eclipse of the Union-Republican Club of Jacksonville as a power faction in Reconstruction Florida.[36] However, few of the secondary accounts have emphasized the structure of the debate that followed the motion to adopt the minority report of the permanent committee on organization. That report had designated Hart as chairman, while the majority report had selected Thomas Osborn. "An animated discussion arose," the *Tallahassee Sentinel* reporter observed, "and a hard fight ensued." Following a brief recess, the debate on this one motion lasted from 3:00 P.M. to 7:00 P.M. of the convention's first day. Hart was defeated by a 19 to 28 margin.[37]

The debate over this issue was more than a factional haggle. Liberty Billings and Green Davidson of Leon County, the radicals who participated in the debate, were forced to choose sides, and while both would have preferred a more radical chairman than either Hart or Osborn, in choosing the latter they presumably were taking the lesser evil. This was the first time black politicians were forced into alignments that could have yielded maximum advantage, but, as was the case later and elsewhere, their position failed to gain them anything. There was nothing in the platform for the freedmen beyond a plank that denounced the tax on them and one that called for a committee to investigate acts of "gross injustice" to all loyal men.[38] Although the convention has been labeled a "mixed multitude" because of the presence of black delegates, these representatives were neither numerous nor especially well accepted by their white counterparts. In fact, not all of the 125 elected representatives attended; some were represented by proxy. Although one unanimous resolution was passed praising Jacksonville's *Florida Union* as an "able exponent" of Republican views and another in support of racial harmony, Billings' motion calling for unsegregated seating on the convention floor was defeated. Nor did the delegates apparently choose to intermingle racially outside the convention hall.[39] Walls' activities were of little importance at this convention, and his reactions and thoughts about it are, of course, unknown. In any event he was settled squarely in the radical ranks of the "mule team" when the constitutional convention delegates gathered in Tallahassee in January 1868.

36. Meador, "Florida Political Parties," pp. 72–73.
37. *Tallahassee Semi-Weekly Floridian*, July 12, 1867; *Tallahassee Sentinel*, July 15, 1867.
38. Ibid.; *American Annual Cyclopaedia and Register of Important Events of the Year 1867*, 7:313.
39. *Tallahassee Sentinel*, July 15, 1867.

Following the platform convention, Republicans returned to their home counties to ready themselves for the crucial battle. For die-hard conservatives around the state, the last half of 1867 was a dismal season. The Pensacola *West Florida Commercial*, despondent over the political future, hoped that by some miracle all Negroes would become extinct under emancipation, a gloomy prospect made even more so by the "consideration that he [the Negro] is . . . under the influence of selfish, scheming, reckless white men."[40] One white Conservative suggested that peace would never come to the South until the national government set aside three or four states (not in the South) for black people only and under black control. "It makes a rebel almost insane with rage to speak of a Negro government in Fla. and all the Southern States."[41] It is ironic to note that George S. Boutwell, the radical Massachusetts congressman, also proposed that the Negroes should be separated; however, he planned to relocate them in South Carolina, Georgia, and Florida.[42]

The constitutional convention was called for January 20, 1868. Walls had been elected to represent Alachua County along with William Cessna and Horatio Jenkins, Jr., a former army officer from Massachusetts who had settled in Gainesville after the war. Few whites of conservative leaning had bothered to vote, following instead the general statewide belief that conservative nonparticipation would somehow cripple radical plans. In the county, the conservative Gainesville *New Era* had acknowledged briefly the candidacy of Garth James, younger brother of William and Henry James, until he indicated that, in his opinion, "the measures for Reconstruction passed by Congress are eminently wise and just."[43]

Struggles and discussions took place in Tallahassee's hotel rooms and bars as well as on the floor of the convention hall.[44] Walls, a member of the Richards-Saunders-Billings faction, "the mule team," played only a minor role in the ongoing proceedings. He did not serve on any committees when the convention was first organized, but he was appointed by the rump convention to its finance committee after the moderates and

40. December 26, 1867.
41. J. Cory, Jr., to Schuyler Colfax, December 25, 1867, J. Cory, Jr., folder.
42. *Congressional Globe*, 38th Cong., 1st sess., pp. 2102–5.
43. September 18, 1867.
44. See works in note 28 for accounts of the 1868 constitutional convention and the reports in the Tallahassee newspapers. See also *Journal of the Proceedings of the Constitutional Convention of the State of Florida Begun . . . on Monday, January 20th, 1868*. Two important recent studies of the constitutional convention are Jerrell H. Shofner, "The Constitution of 1868," and Richard L. Hume, "The 'Black and Tan' Constitutional Conventions of 1867–1869 in Ten Former Confederate States: A Study of Their Membership."

conservatives vacated Tallahassee for Monticello, where they had the opportunity to combine forces.[45] When the moderate-conservative combine gained control in the reorganized convention, Walls was appointed to the militia committee, as was Cessna. Walls' voting record, as evidenced by the roll call on several significant issues, indicates clearly that he remained a "radical" throughout—until the final vote adopting the moderate state constitution. He voted for Daniel Richards as president of the convention; voted for postponement of a discussion of some radical delegates' eligibility to maintain their seats (a question primarily affecting Richards, Saunders, and Billings); defected to vote for Horatio Jenkins, Jr., for president of the reorganized convention (Jenkins was a fellow representative from Alachua County, and the black-white Republican split in the county had not yet opened); voted against the removal of Richards, Saunders, Charles Pearce, and Solon Robinson of the *New York Tribune* and against the seating of the replacement delegates—Hart, Marcellus Stearns, and Richard Wells; but then voted for final adoption of the constitution.[46]

The reasons behind Walls' voting pattern, especially in the reorganized convention, cannot be fully understood. One can account for the obvious shift from "mule team radical" to moderate-conservative supporter, however, and it would appear that his voting reflected the pattern of events that had led up to the convention, and which operated within it. William Watson Davis argued that the 1868 convention in Tallahassee was nothing more than a struggle between two forces—"Negro rule" imposing a "radical" constitution and the valiant white population engaged in determined resistance.[47] This early racist interpretation has been revised by Jerrell H. Shofner in favor of an emphasis upon the political factionalism that operated in the convention. Shofner points to the positive benefits that both races received from the moderate constitution and concludes: "For reasons of their own, the radicals in the Constitutional Convention were unbending in their demands for Negro equality and punishment of ex-Confederates. . . . Native Conservatives, though deprived of participation in the Convention, constituted an important part of Florida's population. They were unwilling to be subjected to domination by northern radicals supported by a Negro electorate. . . . The radical leaders lost because they asked too much and could not accept less since their entire support came from Negroes. . . .

45. *Journal of the Constitutional Convention, 1868*, p. 14.
46. Hume, "The 'Black and Tan' Constitutional Conventions," p. 563.
47. Davis, *Civil War and Reconstruction in Florida*, pp. 491–513.

Unlike the radicals, the moderate Republicans were willing to seek support wherever it could be found."[48]

If the traditional view of the events does not portray accurately the sense of the historical happenings, the revisionist interpretation also does not complete the picture; the truth lies somewhere between these divergent views. If the radicals were "unbending" in their demands for equality, it was because most of the delegates in the radical faction were black. Of twenty-one radicals in the convention, only six were white with two originally from other states. Thus, unless the moderate-conservative combine's major purpose was merely to isolate Daniel Richards and Liberty Billings (the "mule team" leaders who would have "dominated" Florida's Negroes), the answer must be more complex. William Cone, H. Krimminger, J. H. Goss, and Eldredge Ware, the four native white Floridians who were members of the radical faction, share some interesting characteristics that help explain their political leanings, not in terms of Negro domination, but rather as a reaction against former Confederates. These were men who had suffered for their unionist sentiment in the Civil War. Three of them had deserted from the Confederate army, and none was in sound financial condition.[49] Thus these white radicals may have been "unbending" because of their alienation from those southerners who had caused them such misery.

Moreover, only fourteen of the original eighteen blacks in the convention have been identified as radical. The other five men (one black was added to the reorganized convention) were clearly in the conservative ranks. The black radicals, the largest numerical faction, could not have been neutralized or effectively isolated in any way except by a combination of the remaining whites—moderates and conservatives—into a working majority. It should be remembered that at the July Republican platform convention, the radicals had maintained the balance of power and thrown their weight in support of Thomas Osborn, who was more moderate than Ossian Hart. This is clear evidence that the radicals had not been "unbending" at all in their search for support. What is indicated is the view that the constitutional convention was produced by a combination that excluded the black radicals and insured that Florida's constitutional government, in Reconstruction and after, would remain safely in white hands. Thus, it is at least partially true that the factionalism in this convention did center on blacks against whites, but not in the sense suggested by William Watson Davis. Yet the moderate-

48. Shofner, "The Constitution of 1868," pp. 372–73.
49. Hume, "The 'Black and Tan' Constitutional Conventions," p. 557.

conservative versus radical dichotomy tends to cloud the issue. The constitutional convention was not a situation in which moderate Republicans were "willing" to seek support wherever it could be found; rather, these Republicans, remembering that the radicals previously had held the swing vote in a power vacuum, were anxious to seek further white support to prevent a second occurrence of that political position.

Following the constitutional convention, the moderate Republicans hoped to assuage black disappointment by a fence-mending campaign. One example usually cited is that of William Saunders, who left the mule team to further his own career. In joining the moderates, he earned the open enmity of Daniel Richards.[50] Walls also had been a radical member of the mule team who had forsaken it to support the new constitution, but events were to prove that he in particular did not fence-mend wholeheartedly. The proposals advanced in the first sessions of the Florida legislature under the new, moderate constitution by Walls and Henry S. Harmon, his closest political ally and friend in Alachua County, reflected their intent to push for radical improvements. It was probable that, as black politicians, Saunders and Walls realized the futility of hard resistance to moderate aims. If they were concerned about a continuing black presence (themselves in particular) in a white political world, their alternatives were as yet limited. Thus, they surrendered in the 1868 constitutional convention rather than become relegated to obscurity. In fact, one could argue that this course of action was evidence of greater flexibility, not inflexibility, on the radical faction's part. In any event, Walls was able to continue his political career over a longer period of time than was possible for many other blacks who refused to accommodate themselves to political reality.

The political situation after the formal drafting of the new constitution continued to be unstable. The black radicals were unhappy with their treatment at Tallahassee, and, for a time at least, a few hoped that Congress would reject the document. Although bemoaning the advent of a non-existent "radical" Reconstruction, the conservatives rapidly organized themselves into a viable political party seeking to recapture the state government from Republican control. Meanwhile the Republican moderates embarked on their campaign to win the Negro vote. Their program was persuasive; the moderates appealed to the need for party unity against the "rebel" threat. By so doing, they played upon the emotional prejudice of the black people in favor of the party of Lincoln, emancipation, and protection.

50. Shofner, "The Constitution of 1868," p. 373.

This complex political situation continued throughout the spring of 1868. On March 7, Alachua County Republicans met in Gainesville to place in nomination their candidates for the fall election. The twenty-five delegates selected William Cessna as president of the nominating convention, Henry Harmon, John E. Hills, and Albert McKinney as vice presidents, and Horatio Jenkins as secretary. Walls was neither elected nor appointed to any of the convention posts.[51] The nominations were not made without some controversy. Walls and Harmon were chosen for the assembly and Jenkins for the senate only "after a long and interesting debate" in which the three candidates and Cessna were the principal figures. Details of the debate have not been preserved, but the nature of the discussion reasonably may be surmised in light of preceding events at Tallahassee and in Alachua County.

It is likely that Walls and Harmon were unhappy with the end product of the constitutional convention, although they had resolved to support the document and the Republican party. Walls must have been disappointed in the total defeat of the black faction. As a politician and a black, he must have realized the futility of open opposition to the white power structure now firmly established in the state. At the same time, he and Harmon were determined to capture the Alachua County political leadership from Cessna and Jenkins. A compromise was agreed upon by the white and black Republicans to enable the groups to share control of the county. One indication of this was that Harmon, but not Walls, was elected to the Alachua County Republican executive committee, and Cessna, but not Jenkins, was also elected to the same committee. If the merits of the state constitution were discussed at all, the discussion did not change the convention's public position, as various resolutions in behalf of the platform, the principles, and the Republican party were passed.[52]

But it is also interesting to note that at a Republican rally in Newnansville on April 11, Walls, Saunders, and Harmon made "strong speeches endorsing the regular ticket and the Constitution."[53] Jenkins and Cessna, however, were not reported as having attended this rally, even though it was held to counter a large Democratic mass meeting at the county courthouse in Gainesville on the same day. This factionalism so disgusted Garth James, for example, that, by the end of the year, he wrote home to his father that his political opinions "have been growing

51. *Tallahassee Sentinel*, March 19, 1868; (Jacksonville)*Florida Union*, March 14, 1868.
52. (Jacksonville) *Florida Union*, March 14, 1868.
53. Ibid.

more conservative of late." On New Year's Eve he wrote: "White men and negroes alike, whether they come from Massachusetts or South Carolina are all bent on getting the best of each other, and for the last two months since I have had so much to do, in the care of the plantations, I have had a chance to get my fill of the diabolical atmosphere which keeps alive all men of this class. Politically and privately, all men, with but few exceptions down here, are working for one object, namely that of cheating everyone else in order to add a few dollars to their own possessions."[54]

Walls and Harmon apparently were successful in consolidating their control; both men were easy victors in the general elections for the first session of the legislature. Their victims were Samuel Y. Finley and D. McHenry, who lost to Walls and to Harmon by more than 1,000 votes each.[55] On June 8, 1868, Walls and Harmon entered the Florida state legislature's assembly hall as the elected officials from Alachua County.

Walls presented his credentials and was sworn in the following day when a quorum for the conduct of business had been achieved. His first official act as a Florida legislator was to serve on the customary committee appointed by the speaker of the house for the session, William M. Moore of Columbia County, to "wait upon" Governor Harrison Reed. The chief executive was informed that the senate and the house were duly organized and ready to receive his address.

This was the first session under the new constitution, and thus under different conditions than previous meetings of the Florida legislature. The agenda was crowded with measures that underscored the need to forget the war and times past and to forge ahead with railroads, canals, and other internal improvements. The Fourteenth Amendment was passed with little opposition via Marcellus Stearns' resolution.[56]

Walls' performance in the first busy days of the legislative session was undistinguished. He was appointed to serve on the committee for the adoption of the parliamentary procedure for the assembly; he offered a resolution that opened the floor of the assembly to the governor and his cabinet whenever they should appear; and he proposed that Edward M. Cheney be appointed the state printer, a resolution that passed the lower house but failed to get support in the senate.[57] (Cheney eventually

54. Garth James to his father, November 15, December 31, 1868.
55. (Jacksonville)*Florida Union*, May 16, 1868. Samuel Y. Finley was the son of Jesse J. Finley, who was Walls' opponent in the 1874 congressional campaign.
56. *Assembly Journal. A Journal of the Proceedings of the Assembly of the State of Florida, at Its First Session: Begun . . . on Monday, June 8th, 1868*, p. 19.
57. Ibid., pp. 10, 11, 14.

became the printer, however, and Walls later regretted his kindness. As the editor of the *Florida Union*, Cheney became one of his most bitter political enemies.) By the end of his first month, Walls had accomplished little more; he had become a member of a relatively unimportant standing committee—printing—and had engineered the fifty-four paperweights and ink sandboxes that appeared on each legislator's desk. He did sponsor a bill, introduced on July 8, that empowered county clerks and court clerks to practice law in Florida. It was read twice and referred to the judiciary committee on July 10. Five days later, the committee reported a revised version of Walls' bill.[58] The basic difference in the two bills was the restriction that clerks could practice law only in the lower courts. Although the committee's debates on this particular bill are not recorded, no doubt Walls realized that his bill would insure that blacks who became county clerks could then practice law in Florida. The changed bill removed the potential of practice in higher courts for black men who had not yet been admitted to the bar.

Another example of the legislature's attitude on the subject of Negro rights came to the fore on July 14, when John Simpson of Marion County introduced House Bill 28, which provided that the people of Florida "without distinction" were to enjoy public hotels. As the bill was the only one of this first session of the legislature to provide specifically for civil rights, a detailed examination of the bill's trip through the legislature is in order.

Number 28 was referred, on the day of its introduction, to the judiciary committee. When it was reported out, it carried both a majority report favoring its passage and a minority report that recited the classical arguments of the day opposed to black advancement. Signed by George Raney and Daniel C. McKinnon, the minority report opposed the bill because it would negate "the inherent rights of a free people and [was] contrary to the genius of republican government." Bill 28 was also felt to be an attack on private property, "calculated to injure the peace and good feeling of public Society." McKinnon and Raney argued that it makes "a crime of that which by its nature is not a crime, and opens the door for disturbances where none would otherwise occur. . . . It is therefore earnestly recommended that the said bill do not pass; the correctness, justice, and wisdom of which recommendation we leave time to decide."[59]

Although not killed by the judiciary committee, the bill continued to

58. Ibid., pp. 49, 83–89.
59. Ibid., pp. 129–30.

face opposition in the assembly. A motion for "indefinite postpone-ment," offered by F. J. Harris of Marion County, was quickly countered by Harmon, who moved to table the Harris motion. This parliamentary tangle was resolved when Harmon's proposal was turned down, 20 to 23, and was followed by a 19 to 24 defeat of Harris' resolution. Walls voted for the Harmon measure in fear of a final defeat of the bill; he then voted against the Harris motion to lay the whole matter aside.

On July 23, the day after the favorable committee report reached the floor, a new obstacle was presented. McKinnon, still determined to void the civil rights measure, proposed a resolution calling for a joint legisla-tive committee of seven members—three from the senate and four from the lower house—to examine all the pending bills of both houses and to recommend for further consideration only those bills whose passage was deemed absolutely essential in the ongoing session. According to McKinnon's proposal, all other bills were to be delayed until the joint committee's recommendations were disposed of.[60] Walls managed to have this motion tabled.

Finally, Simpson's bill passed the lower house by a 25 to 18 vote.[61] Two days later, it was introduced in the senate and was referred to the committee on state affairs. On July 29, it was reported favorably from committee. On the last day of the month the bill died a quiet parliamen-tary death, having been postponed indefinitely. This almost matched the observation of the Tallahassee *Weekly Floridian*, which had noted the arrival of the civil rights measure into the senate and commented only that "it is likely to remain" in committee.[62] This bill, fought for with some success in its early stages but doomed to defeat in that era, stands in ironic contrast to the summary of the first session of the legislature offered by the Republican newspaper in the capital city: "The Legisla-ture is working faithfully at its duties of remodelling the laws, to adapt them to the new state of affairs, and so to fashion every part that the peace, happiness, and security of all the citizens will be promoted by them. . . . Numerous bills for the enlarging and improving of water courses to make them navigable have been considered. Schemes for draining and reclaiming overflowed lands, opening canals, and building railroads have been acted upon."[63]

60. Ibid., pp. 132–35.
61. Ibid., p. 139.
62. *Senate Journal. Journal of the Senate, for the First Session, Fifteenth Legislature, of the State of Florida, Begun . . . on the Eighth Day of June . . . One Thousand Eight Hundred and Sixty Eight*, pp. 129, 139, 169, 186; (Tallahassee) *Weekly Floridian*, July 28, 1868.
63. *Tallahassee Sentinel*, June 30, 1868.

The local newspaper and, indeed, the white citizenry of the state may have felt satisfaction, or at least relief, in the discovery that the Florida legislature confined itself to matters of railway construction, land reclamation, and the opening of canals. For the black legislators, the session proved a deep disappointment. After the close of the session on August 6, several Negro assemblymen remained huddled on the assembly floor in an informal and impromptu caucus. The results of the session just ended were discussed, and the politicians who gathered openly laid the blame for the lack of racial progress on "conservatives, weak-kneed Republicans, and perverse colored people."

According to Charles Pearce, the black state senator from the eighth district, "every appeal . . . has been voted down by these conservatives and weak-kneed Republicans." He suggested that blacks would have to turn inward for support if those Republicans "who have ridden into power on [conservative] shoulders" continued to join with Democrats in "oppressing" black people. Pearce castigated those who had "either shirked their responsibility or voted with the conservatives." The result was that "southern loyalists and the colored [had] very little to hope for."[64] This view of the political situation, in describing black frustration on the floor of the legislature, reaffirms the idea that black politicians were neither uncritical nor unaware of Republican lack of commitment to them in Reconstruction Florida. Their problem was a lack of alternatives.

At this same meeting Walls continued his feud with the white party faction of Alachua County, vehemently denying that William Cessna had exercised any control over his actions on the assembly floor. He denied being "influenced and manipulated," and he defended his or any black man's right to "a bold and independent stand." He noted that any Negro who took such a position ran the risk of being labeled as under the control of "outside influences." There were those, however, who did "not care for these aspersions, and would show it in the next campaign."[65]

The extra session of the legislature in 1868 was not scheduled to meet until early November. It is impossible to tell what Walls did in the intervening months. Perhaps he spent some time in Newnansville with "Ella," as his wife Helen was apparently called. In any event, he returned to Tallahassee on November 3 for the Republican state nominating convention. He was named to the important committee on creden-

64. (Tallahassee) *Weekly Floridian*, August 11, 1868.
65. Ibid.

tials, perhaps in recognition of his rising position in Florida politics, or because moderate Republicans still were trying to placate Walls in their fence-mending campaign.

By this time Walls had broken with the "mule team," as had William Saunders. Liberty Billings, a member of the original radical faction, arrived at the nominating convention with a contesting delegation from Leon County. His opponent was Saunders. The dispute was turned over to Walls' committee, and the Saunders delegation was seated. The convention renominated Charles Hamilton for the Forty-first Congress, and as the incumbent he had no serious opposition.[66] Eventually, Saunders announced himself as an independent candidate for the congressional seat, but blacks, despite their disaffection, did not yet choose to bolt the Republican party.

The Saunders campaign pointed out what may well have been the basic problem for Negro politicians during Reconstruction. An overwhelming number of freedmen simply refused to resist the Republican party, the party of emancipation. Because of this, black leaders were forced to remain within regular party channels to insure political survival. It is true that some Republicans may have become concerned over the potential Negro alternative of bolting their party, and therefore they may have felt the need to proffer more offices to blacks. Whether the situation was real or imaginary, Josiah Walls happened to become the man in Florida who was to benefit greatly from this applied political pressure.

Following the nominating convention, the legislature reconvened for the purpose of selecting as presidential electors James D. Green, John W. Butler, and Robert Meacham. This session soon assumed more significance. On November 6, Horatio Jenkins presented charges calling for the impeachment of Harrison Reed. The governor, a sometimes cantankerous figure in Florida politics, never maintained a strong alliance with any of the Republican factions in the state, and this was the first of four attempts to remove him from office. Walls' actions in the session indicate that Reed had support among Florida Negroes. The legislature had voted for a bill Governor Reed considered unconstitutional; it called for $500 in annual salary, $5 per diem, 10 cents a mile in travel allowance, and an additional $5 for each twenty miles of travel to and from Tallahassee. Walls' compromise motion would have reduced the per diem rate for legislators, but it lost out on the assembly floor. The

66. (Jacksonville) *Florida Union*, November 9, 1868.

revenue measure passed over the governor's veto, although Walls and other black legislators voted to sustain the governor.[67]

Walls then returned to Alachua County for the remainder of the year. He purchased eighty acres of land near Newnansville on November 25, 1868.[68] He also turned his attention to enlarging his political fortunes as well by announcing as a candidate for the state senate to replace Horatio Jenkins. Jenkins, who had been briefly commissioned as a county judge, soon was impeached from that office through the efforts of Harrison Reed. For Walls, that meant another step forward in the consolidation of his power within Alachua County.

The December election again raised to the surface the deep factional splits in county politics. Walls' chief opponents were Cessna and conservative candidate James H. Roper, an educator and influential figure in county politics. On New Year's Eve, Garth James wrote to his parents that Jenkins "feels undoubtedly very badly. . . . He is a poor broken down adventurer now, and a warning to all men who do not make some attempt to serve something higher than themselves." James also described the Walls-Cessna-Roper contest as "very agitating" and "one that called in play all the elements good and bad the community possessed."[69] In the election itself, Walls made good his public threat to Cessna that some people would not forget the "aspersions" Cessna had cast on Walls' character. Walls defeated Roper handily in Alachua County, 525 to 352, while completely submerging Cessna. The Levy County vote, of which Roper received the majority, was not enough to offset Walls' wide margin.[70] Walls had gained control. He also increased his landholdings at this time, by purchasing another parcel of land from James Saunders for $500 on December 22.[71] Walls thus began 1869 headed for the Florida senate.

Charles Pearce, an ordained minister in the African Methodist Church in Florida and a power in black prayer meetings and politics, presented the new senator's credentials to the senate on January 7. That body quickly became embroiled in debate about who was to succeed William Gleason as president of the senate. Gleason had resigned in the wake of

67. *A Journal of the Proceedings of the Joint Convention of the Florida Legislature . . . November 3, 1868, and of the Senate and Assembly of the State of Florida, at an Extraordinary Session of the Legislature, Convened November 3, 1868*, pp. 3, 40.

68. Deed Book G, p. 701, Clerk of the Circuit Court, Alachua County Courthouse.

69. Garth James to his parents, December 31, 1868.

70. Official canvass, *Florida Executive Department Journal*, November 1865–December 1872.

71. Deed Book H, p. 335, Clerk of the Circuit Court, Alachua County Courthouse.

the first unsuccessful impeachment attempt against Reed; earlier, he had resigned as lieutenant governor and had declared himself governor in the abortive coup against Reed. That resignation raised a constitutional question as to his legitimate right to remain as head of the senate. Gleason ended the resulting controversy by resigning voluntarily prior to possible court action. Walls entered the debate by introducing a resolution calling for the recognition of Pearce as president. Pearce had replaced Gleason in the president's chair during the previous session in November. However, a substitute resolution that ignored Pearce's efforts of the past was also presented, and in a compromise, Walls withdrew his own motion. The substitute resolution was then also withdrawn from the floor, and the senate proceeded to an election for the post. As expected, factional interests surfaced, and the issue was not resolved until the tenth ballot, when J. M. Krimminger of the twelfth district defeated Pearce and William J. Purman of the third district, a leader of the white faction opposed to Harrison Reed. The senate then moved to organize itself for business. One indication of the diffuse attitudes among the senators was the fact that even Walls received some support on the third vote.[72]

The record is unclear concerning the committee assignments Walls received in this session of the legislature; his name does not appear on the original list of the members' appointments to the senate's standing committees. He was chosen for two special committees—codes of practice (revision of parliamentary procedure) and code of criminal laws. He also apparently served at least part of the session on the important judiciary and education committees.[73]

Walls' efforts during the session seem to have been relatively unimpressive. He presented a series of petitions from the citizens of Levy County and sponsored a bill that permanently established their county seat. While a member of the education committee, he voted for the bill that established a uniform system of common schools and a university in Florida. This was a bill similar to that which had suffered defeat in the first session of the legislature, an event much criticized in the caucus that followed the end of the first session. This time the bill was reported from committee favorably on January 25, 1869, and it was passed by the senate the following day.[74]

72. *Senate Journal. A Journal of the Proceedings of the Senate of the State of Florida at the Second Session of the Legislature, Begun . . . January 5th, A. D., 1869*, pp. 18, 20–21.

73. Ibid., pp. 26–28.

74. Ibid., p. 96.

It was later, in the extra session, that Walls in the senate and Harmon in the assembly launched a dual attack in an attempt to gain some positive legislation for the black people of Florida. The extra session began on June 8, called by the governor to provide a law for uniform taxation, to secure legislation that would insure completion of a railroad to the western boundary of the state, and to ratify the Fifteenth Amendment.[75] On June 11, the senate voted to delay its vote on ratification until the assembly had indicated its choice. The assembly did so that same day, ratifying the amendment by a 2 to 1 margin. The amendment was submitted to the senate's judiciary committee and was reported favorably; a minority report, however, accompanied it to the senate floor. The minority report, signed by William H. Kendricks of the twenty-third district, adhered to traditional states' rights logic in opposing ratification. Kendricks pointed out that the Constitution reserved suffrage qualifications to the states. The majority report was adopted by a close vote, 12 to 9.[76]

Despite conservative opposition to black rights, Walls and Harmon pressed for legislation for their race. In the senate, Walls introduced a bill that would have committed the state to the protection of its citizens from illegal violence. There was much violence in Florida at this time, as the Ku Klux Klan was at the peak of its terrorist campaign.[77] His bill would have laid upon the state militia responsibility for curbing the Klan. The bill was referred to a special committee of the senate composed of Kendricks, McCaskill, Cruse, Meacham, and Walls. Although this committee voted in favor of the bill, the minority report signed by Kendricks and McCaskill stated that "the subject embraced therein is amply secured by existing laws" and recommended indefinite postponement.[78] The senate agreed.

In the assembly Harmon was even more outspoken in favor of Negro rights. He introduced a bill to protect people traveling on public conveyances. The bill was assigned to the judiciary committee, and the minority report, signed by McKinnon, reflected white sentiments about

75. *Senate Journal. A Journal of the Proceedings of the Senate of the State of Florida at an Extra Session of the Legislature, Begun . . . Tuesday, June 8th, A. D., 1869*, pp. 5–6. The railroad issue, which eventually developed into the Swepson-Littlefield fraud, has received sufficient attention elsewhere as to its manipulations and the involvement of various politicians. In passing, however, it must be noted that Walls does not appear to have been connected with this particular fraud in any way. There is evidence that he played an important role, and a rewarding one, in another railroad scandal in the state.

76. Ibid., pp. 22, 29.

77. Ralph L. Peek, "Aftermath of Military Reconstruction, 1868–1869."

78. *Senate Journal, 1869*, extra session, p. 64.

social equality. McKinnon argued that the intention of the bill was "to enforce indirectly social equality upon the people. . . . We also further maintain that it is not in keeping with good taste, for any class of persons . . . to force their society upon another class." He affirmed the right of railroads to discriminate on the basis of color; however, he did think that color discrimination should be accompanied by lower rates. "But it seems that the advocates, or at all events, the framer of this bill [Harmon] is not content with these equitable terms, but persistently insists upon having not only equal, but the *same* accommodations." Harmon's bill was defeated in the assembly.[79]

Thus, by the end of this legislative session, the pattern of racial politics in Florida's Reconstruction was complete. Walls, Harmon, and the other elected black officials voted for the various measures calling for railroad construction, canal building, and appropriations for other ventures that the white power elite desired. Moreover, in the case of Walls at least, a black politician also remained responsive to his entire electorate, in voting, presenting petitions of the citizens, and sponsoring countywide bills as well as relief measures for individuals. His measures for the rights of black people were rebuffed in return. Black political discontent was clearly expressed even if black political alternatives were not. Proscription of black political leverage, first appearing in the constitutional convention of 1868, was continued in the state legislative sessions. William Saunders' unsuccessful attempt to run an independent campaign for the congressional seat of Charles Hamilton proved that black leaders were not powerful enough to carry out an all-black independent political canvass. Thus, they were forced to continue within the ranks of the Republican party and therein exercise at least some measure of influence in their own behalf.

For Walls, the entrance into Florida politics had proved auspicious. In Alachua County he had established a firm power base and had indeed become a force in Florida, at least as a spokesman for his race. Because he could advance no farther in state circles, it seemed natural that he would in time set his sights for higher office.

79. *Assembly Journal. A Journal of the Proceedings of the Assembly of the State of Florida, at an Extra Session Begun . . . on Tuesday, June 8th, 1869*, pp. 27–28, 32.

3

Silas Niblack and the
Campaigns for Congress,
1870–1872

POLITICAL conditions in Florida began to change rapidly in the early
1870s. Republican expectations of permanent control of the state government quickly dissipated into a struggle for survival. Two developments forced the moderate Republican leadership to consider nominating a Negro for a statewide office. First was the increased violence and
terrorist activity that swept Florida during this period, and the other was
the rapid advance made by the rising tide of Conservative votes in state
elections. Past performance, unmodified by these new political currents,
would have negated the chances of any black politician for higher office.
Because of these currents, however, Josiah Walls was nominated and
elected to the House of Representatives.

Terrorist violence in Florida and the rest of the South has been
alternately romanticized, excused, and condemned. Many of the earlier
accounts of Reconstruction tended to minimize the amount of violence
that took place, while others stated flatly that the reported cases were
exaggerated.[1] More recently, George R. Bentley referred to "tales"
of atrocities, although he also admitted there was "considerable truth in
the postwar reports of violence and cruelty." Bentley maintained, however, that the Bureau agents were "frequently prone to exaggerate the
violence they encountered and to report rumors without determining
their authenticity."[2] To others, the terrorist organizations (generically
considered as the Ku Klux Klan) were symbols of a violent and

1. See, for example, James Ford Rhodes, *History of the United States from the Compromise
of 1850*, 5:563, and Robert Selph Henry, *The Story of Reconstruction*, pp. 84–85.
2. *History of the Freedmen's Bureau*, p. 110.

confirmed disrespect for lawful government, a view most often expressed by blacks and Republican whites. It was "either a glorious or sinister symbol," wrote Francis B. Simkins in summary of the Klan, "for the arousal of issues of race, religion, and patriotism in which all Americans . . . are vitally concerned."[3]

Only the most recent scholarship has suggested that postwar politics best explains the pattern and practices of the Klan or Klan-inspired groups.[4] The violent activities of the Young Men's Democratic Clubs in Florida demonstrate the political reasons behind the "Republican decline" following its 1868 zenith.[5] These clubs, composed mostly of young, white Floridians, intended to capture control of the state government for the Conservatives in the 1870 campaign. To that end, in many Florida counties bands of men rode to intimidate, burn out, and sometimes murder those whose votes were not in accord with their aims. In Alachua County alone there were nineteen murders and numerous less violent frays during the period 1867–71.[6] And as one contemporary in the county noted, most, if not all, involved Republican victims.[7] Another Alachua County resident testified that there were a half-dozen secret societies in the county whose sole objective was "to use force or violence to prevent certain parties from exerting too great an influence with the colored population . . . [and] to be prepared to do so effectually and secretly."[8]

One white Republican who suffered because of his leadership in Alachua County was Leonard G. Dennis, a Massachusetts carpetbagger who had settled there after the war. Better known as the "Little Giant," Dennis quickly became an acknowledged party leader and was elected to replace Walls in the state assembly. He and Walls engaged in a prolonged battle, spanning the entire period of Reconstruction, for party leadership in the county. Dennis received several notices threatening his life, and Walls himself narrowly escaped being shot during a political rally. In any event, it was in these violent surroundings that Republicans, black and white, carried on their political activities and intra-party disputes.

The Conservative party itself had made substantial progress in voter

3. "New Viewpoints of Southern Reconstruction," p. 50.
4. Allen W. Trelease, *White Terror: The Ku Klux Conspiracy and Southern Reconstruction*, passim.
5. Peek, "Aftermath of Military Reconstruction," pp. 123–24.
6. U. S. Congress, *Joint Select Committee on the Condition of Affairs in the Late Insurrectionary States*, 42d Cong., 2d sess., *House Document 22*, vol. 13, passim; Emma B. Eveleth to E. P. Smith, December 29, 1869, American Missionary Archives.
7. Eveleth to Smith, December 30, 1868, American Missionary Archives.
8. Testimony of Frank Myers, November 11, 1871, *House Document 22*, p. 156.

registration and political organization by 1870. Although substantially similar to the antebellum Democratic party, it had adopted the Conservative label in an effort to appeal to older Whigs and to create a clear alternative to "radical" Republicanism.[9] A special census conducted in 1868 by the Conservative *Tallahassee Weekly Floridian* cited the rise in Conservative registrants and predicted their party would sweep the 1870 elections.[10] It was obvious to many Republicans that without some strategic maneuvering to hold voters in line, the Conservative predictions would easily become political reality. In an effort to maintain their hold on the state government, the moderate Republican leadership at last was forced to come to the black voters with concrete rewards. Their sense of urgency had been heightened by William Saunders' independent race against Charles Hamilton in 1868. Although Saunders had fared poorly, his political tactics aroused additional fears that Negroes would desert in large numbers. That, of course, was the precise desire of the Conservatives, who in fact had encouraged Saunders to contest Hamilton. They hoped to benefit from a thorough splintering of the Republican party. All these factors enabled Walls' ambition for higher office to merge nicely with the Republican decision that a black man should be nominated for one.

The Republican nominating convention met in Gainesville on August 19, 1870. Delegates from all over the state crowded into town, filling the available rooms in hotels and boarding houses. Incorporated only the year before, Gainesville was chosen for the convention because of its central location. Not only were the homes of its 3,500 residents scattered "over about 500 acres in the most ingenious disorder," but the courthouse (the convention site) was hardly large enough for this gathering. The reporter covering the convention for the *Tallahassee Sentinel* could not resist a detailed and sarcastic description of it: "It is in the last stages of structural decay, and some aspiring artist has taken occasion to render its dilapidation still more hideous by attempting the production of a graveyard scene, to which is adjoined a prison, on a portion of the walls. The aptness of the illustration, when compared with the surrounding objects, is only excelled by the ability of the artist in the execution of his design."[11]

Into this hot and crowded hall some 300 Republicans, including

9. Davis, *Civil War and Reconstruction in Florida*, pp. 519–20.
10. June 30, 1868.
11. August 20, 1870. The *Tallahassee Sentinel* carried a complete account of the Republican nominating convention.

"sham delegates and duplicates," met to select candidates for lieutenant governor and congressman. The important Republican leaders all attended, and Governor Reed delivered the inaugural address. During several preconvention caucuses on the evening of August 18, it had been decided that Charles Hamilton's seat in the House of Representatives would go to a Negro, although the candidate himself had not been chosen. Despite calls for party unity, most notably in an introductory speech by Alva A. Knight (a political hack who had been rewarded for his loyalty to Reed by an appointment as judge of the fourth judicial circuit in 1868), factions struggled from the outset for control.

The first skirmish occurred over the choice for permanent chairman. As the chief legislative representative from Alachua County, Walls had been selected temporary chairman. In that capacity, he named the committee on permanent organization charged with nominating the permanent officers of the convention. This committee reported back the names of Knight as chairman, and Horatio Jenkins and W. D. Johnson as secretaries. Knight's selection provoked opposition. William J. Purman, state senator and head of a West Florida faction in the convention, objected strenuously on the grounds that Knight was not even an official delegate. Because the regular delegate was present, Purman argued that Knight had no legitimate voice in the proceedings. He was challenged by Jenkins, who recalled that in 1868 at the Republican nominating convention at Tallahassee, Ossian B. Hart of Jacksonville had been chosen under the same conditions. Alva Knight's status as an alternate was of no consequence. Purman continued to insist that Judge Knight withdraw, although the latter continued to refuse. The deadlock was broken when Thomas Wentworth sponsored a motion, passed unanimously, selecting Walls as permanent chairman. Jenkins and Johnson were then confirmed as secretaries.

Despite the August heat and crowded quarters, the delegates moved to meet in closed session to avoid interference from Conservative onlookers. The convention then proceeded to the nomination of a Republican candidate to Congress. The first informal ballot indicated just how the factions lined up. First, despite Republican professions to the contrary, Charles Hamilton retained a large and important block of delegates in support of his renomination. Hamilton had stated prior to the convention that he would not press his claims to the nomination if party unity would be jeopardized.[12] His supporters were led by William Purman.

12. Hamilton's statement, however, was quoted a week after the convention, *ibid.*, August 27, 1870.

United States Sen. Thomas Osborn led a faction pledged to Robert Meacham, an ex-slave from Tallahassee. Osborn hoped Meacham would be able to swing the black voters of Florida away from their loyalty to Governor Reed. If Meacham were chosen, Osborn then would have a leading voice in the state government's internal affairs as well as complete control of federal patronage, which until this time he had had to share with Hamilton.

Most of the black delegates were unaligned and divided among themselves. At the end of the first formal ballot Jonathan Gibbs, Charles Pearce, Henry Harmon, and Walls received support; Walls polled the fewest votes. The next eight ballots did little to alter the situation, as there was only a small shift of votes. Then Charles Pearce, observing the need for a single Negro candidate, withdrew from the race and threw his support to Walls, and as a result the latter became a serious contender.

However, Meacham was but two votes short of the needed majority, and the race settled down to a choice of him, Walls, or Hamilton. The factions were clearly demarcated—the Osborn group was behind Meacham, the Purman wing supported Hamilton, and the independent black delegates were beginning to form behind Walls. Gibbs and Harmon still received token support. Before another ballot could be taken, a near riot broke out on the convention floor. It was discovered that Purman had attempted to vote as an alternate delegate from the wrong district. This was noted and, of course, wildly objected to by the Osbornites. The floor degenerated into a "perfect uproar with shouts for the various candidates." Meanwhile, on the rostrum "Walls brought down his gavel for order with a tremendous slam, and away went all the candles on the stand, scattering grease on everybody's clothes, and causing a general stampede of those men near the stand."[13] During the confusion, the Osborn faction tried to employ a little trickery to win the nomination for Meacham. He needed just two more votes, and it was hoped that Jenkins, the recording secretary, would surreptitiously add the votes and announce the results. The plan failed because Hamilton, Pearce, and Gibbs all demanded another ballot and clean voting slips to insure an honest count. At this point "the whole assembly rose to their feet, and for a time, the fiercest recrimination and demonstration was indulged in by the conflicting elements, and fears were entertained of an unpleasant collision." The black delegates then closed ranks completely behind Walls. First, Harmon renounced his candidacy and declared for Walls, and Gibbs and Pearce followed suit. Many of Hamilton's support-

13. (Tallahassee) *Weekly Floridian*, August 23, 1870.

ers then also switched and, on the eleventh ballot, Walls carried the nomination. As one newspaper observer pointed out, "Walls was now the ascending luminary and his fortune was made."[14]

Race, not party maneuvers, pushed Walls on the road to Washington. Not race in the sense that he was the Negroes' "natural choice" for the honor, but rather in the sense that Negroes alone affirmed his candidacy and then forced the white Republicans of Florida to accede to it.[15] Whites might have determined that a Negro was going to Congress: Negroes determined that the man going would be Josiah T. Walls.

The convention did attempt to heal the wounds opened by the fight for the nomination. On the motion of Judge Knight, Walls' nomination was made unanimous, giving rise to "nearly half an hour [of] the wildest excitement and demonstrations of favor for the successful candidate." Spurred on by his friends, the new candidate strode to the front of the hall and made a short acceptance speech. He expressed thanks for "the unspeakable honor" conferred upon him, although he felt "too much the subject of pleasurable excitement" to do even that in proper fashion. Declining to make a lengthy speech, Walls vowed that he would accomplish what he could, and hoped that "through mistake or otherwise" he should "never be guilty of an action that would make them regret their choice." Charles Hamilton, called to the podium to congratulate Walls, professed that he "had the least possible reason to regret his own defeat." Charles Pearce praised the victorious "gentleman of such excellent promise and tried Republicanism," while Henry Harmon, Walls' political shadow, announced that no better man could have been chosen. Harmon promised to campaign "side-by-side" with the candidate, and he challenged any two Conservatives who wished to debate Walls and himself on the relative merits of parties and principles.

It fell to Jonathan Gibbs to reflect upon the true impact of the nomination. He cogently declared it "not only a vindication of the honor and faith of the Republican party," but also a marked triumph for the Negro race in Florida. "This was the great point sought after and gained." William Purman closed the session by pledging his support to Walls, but none of the Osbornites, including Robert Meacham, came forward to acknowledge the victor.

The convention then turned its attention to the nomination for lieutenant governor, considered by many delegates to be the most crucial business of the entire meeting. One reporter covering the convention had

14. *Tallahassee Sentinel*, August 20, 1870.
15. Richardson, *The Negro in the Reconstruction of Florida*, p. 178.

earlier predicted: "Most of the delegates are beginning to see that the matter of prime importance to the State is the election of a good man to the office of Lieutenant-Governor, and on this point we think the real struggle will take place." A real struggle already had taken place in the balloting for congressman, but again the various factions split behind several candidates. Although Charles Pearce appeared to be the independent black choice, the nominee was going to be white. The Osbornites favored Horatio Jenkins, while Purman's faction supported Samuel T. Day, a Florida-unionist from Columbia County. The independent black delegates swung in behind Day, in repayment for the shift from Hamilton to Walls, and he won easily on the second ballot. In another display of unity and goodwill, the Day nomination also was made unanimous and was received by "a perfect storm of joyous excitement and applause." The state Republican executive committee, to which Walls had been appointed in February, was empowered to draft the party platform for the campaign, and then the convention adjourned.

During the postpolitical celebration, a few instances of "pleasurable excitement" occurred; in one, a Conservative who objected to Republican frivolity was beaten by some of the white delegates in a Gainesville hotel room, and a minor fracas took place. The results of the convention seemed mixed; the Negroes had gained a candidate in Walls, and the Purman faction had secured the nomination of Day. But the critical weakness of the party still remained despite the superficial displays of unity. The factions were unable to resolve their differences permanently, even though confronted by a serious threat to their control.

Walls' Conservative opponent was Silas L. Niblack of Lake City. A Confederate veteran, former slaveowner, and close friend of ex-Senator David Levy Yulee, Niblack won the congressional bid at the Conservative convention in Tallahassee with only slight opposition from Garth James.[16] From the Conservative point of view, the lieutenant governor's race also was more crucial than the congressional contest. If they could elect the lieutenant governor and at the same time sweep the state legislature, it might prove possible to impeach Harrison Reed. On the other hand, as David S. Walker, Conservative governor during presidential Reconstruction, pointed out, a Democratic congressman could do little in a Republican House of Representatives, assuming that he even would be allowed to take his seat.[17] Moreover, many Conservatives

16. *Tallahassee Sentinel*, September 3, 1870.
17. David S. Walker to David Levy Yulee, June 9, 1870, mss. box 18, David Levy Yulee Papers.

felt that the Negroes would never support Samuel Day, nor would white Republicans support Josiah Walls. If that were true, then a Conservative party victory seemed assured.[18]

Walls embarked on his campaign fully confident of success. In his speeches, he continued to challenge his opponent to a debate. One of the early issues raised by the Conservatives was that Walls, as an ex-slave, was ill equipped to be a congressman, while Niblack had all the advantages which education and experience would allow. Walls replied to the charge by an open letter in which he offered to debate his opponent in any or all of several north Florida counties. He added that he would "freely waive delicacy upon the subject of the superior advantages which your birth, education, and experience give you [Niblack] and feel assured that in your thorough gentlemanliness you will waive the same."[19] The attacks on his "previous condition" continued, however, and Walls at last resorted, in a second letter published only a week after he received the nomination, to disclaiming that he was born in slavery.[20] Niblack also chided him for retaining his state senatorial seat while running for Congress, and Walls resigned on September 9, 1870.[21]

His campaign stops included St. Marks, Marianna, Live Oak, Monticello, and Gainesville. At Marianna on October 18, he suffered a recurrence of the eye trouble incurred in the war,[22] but he was well enough nine days later to speak at a rally in Gainesville. Here again Walls criticized Niblack's failure to debate the issues, attributing it to a large "amount of pusilanimity [*sic*]" in the character of his opponent. If it were not cowardice, Walls claimed, Niblack either "had a thorough misconception of the confirmed ignorance of his adherents, and did not desire a candid expression of the merits of both political organizations," or else he was "sneaking around like a snail . . . afraid to meet the issues of the day openly and before the public." Walls' attacks stirred the bipartisan crowd and threatened trouble. After the speech-making, a group of Conservatives challenged a Negro passing out Republican literature near the courthouse. Shots were fired and, while no one was hurt, a bullet missed Walls by inches.[23]

Early in November, Walls, Henry Harmon, and Governor Reed were en route to a political rally on the St. Johns River on board the steamer

18. (Tallahassee) *Weekly Floridian*, August 23, 1870.
19. *Tallahassee Sentinel*, October 8, 1870.
20. Ibid., August 27, 1870.
21. Ibid., October 1, 1870.
22. Ibid., October 22, 1870.
23. Ibid., November 5, 1870.

Oklawaha. When Walls and Harmon were refused accommodations in the first-class cabin, they were forced to spend their time outside on deck. They were joined by the governor, who said he would not part company with his companions. The *Oklawaha* was a Hart Line steamer, owned by Hubbard Hart, a brother of Ossian B. Hart, a prominent Jacksonville Republican. Although the cabin looked like "a temporary shanty set up on an oversized rowboat,"[24] the incident was condemned by one Republican newspaper for denying to Walls and Harmon "decent civility on account of color, under a Constitution, too, which declares that there shall be no discrimination on account of color."[25]

The November 8 election was close and newspapers differed in their early returns. According to the Conservative *Tallahassee Weekly Floridian*, the Conservatives had won by a majority of 402 votes in the lieutenant governor's race and 371 votes in the Walls-Niblack contest. Their returns also showed the party had won a majority in both houses of the legislature.[26] From Clay County, Ambrose Hart wrote that the state had been "turned upside down with politics and the election." He also reported that his district had elected three solid Conservatives to the legislature.[27] On December 31, the *Tallahassee Sentinel* carried the state board of canvassers' official count. It showed that Walls had beaten Niblack by 627 votes, 12,437 to 11,810. The board had thrown out the returns from nine Florida counties and three Duval County precincts. According to the Conservatives, had these returns been counted they would have reversed the election.

Meanwhile, Niblack had already initiated steps to contest the results. On November 18, 1870, he wrote for advice to Edward L'Engle, later president of the Florida Central Railroad and a prominent Conservative attorney from Jacksonville: "A dispatch from Tallahassee expresses the opinion that our ticket is elected by a majority ranging from 250 to 400. This is an estimated result. I am of the opinion it is correct. But we all know the returns have to go through the hands of the Rads in Tallahassee before the final count is made. I will therefore leave this matter to [your] judgement . . . and if you think it advisable to commence legal proceedings, you are fully authorized to do so."[28]

24. C. Bradford Mitchell, "Paddle-Wheel Inboard: Some of the History of Oklawaha River Steamboating and of the Hart Line."
25. *Palatka Herald*, n.d., quoted in *Tallahassee Sentinel*, November 19, 1870.
26. November 22, 1870.
27. Ambrose Hart to mother, November 11, 1870, Hart Letters.
28. Silas L. Niblack to Edward M. L'Engle, November 18, 1870, Edward M. L'Engle Papers, mss. box 3, folder 49.

The state board of canvassers was composed of secretary of state Jonathan Gibbs, attorney general Sherman Conant, and state treasurer Robert Gamble. Conant and Gibbs were Republicans, while Gamble was an old-line Whig who had joined the Conservative party. The board began its count November 29, before returns had been received from all the electoral districts in Conservative strongholds. The Conservatives were positive that the official result, which required only a majority approval of the board, would invalidate enough of their party's votes to insure a Republican victory. William Bloxham, the Conservative candidate for lieutenant governor, and Gamble attempted to block the premature count by obtaining an injunction, from Judge P. W. White of the second judicial district, in restraint of the official count and publication of the results. The board ignored the injunction as a violation of the Enforcement Act of 1870, which prohibited interference with election officials. Although White eventually was indicted for his part in the controversy, the charges were dropped and Walls was declared the winner.[29]

Shortly after the first of the year, Niblack served notice he intended to contest the election. In a brief dated January 14, 1871, he outlined his case. Claiming that he had in fact garnered a majority of votes cast, Niblack argued that he had received 156 votes from the Yellow Bluff precinct, 31 from Mayport, and 28 from Baldwin, all in Duval County and all thrown out by the board. Furthermore, the state election officials had rejected 47 Conservative votes from the Fort Ogden precinct in Manatee County, and 925 more from Brevard, Calhoun, Monroe, Sumter, Suwannee, and Taylor counties. Only 78 Walls votes in these areas had been disallowed. If all these rejected votes had been included in the count, Niblack contended, he would have been the winner over Walls by 435 votes.

The contestant also charged that several Republican votes should have been thrown out. The returns from the Escambia navy yard were illegal as the yard was federal property and not under state jurisdiction; the downtown Jacksonville precinct had closed at 9:00 P.M., long after sundown; and some returns from heavily Republican precincts in Alachua and Columbia counties were filed improperly and lacked the required signatures of the local canvassing boards. However, these latter charges would not be pressed by Niblack if Walls would forego "the

29. Ralph L. Peek, "Election of 1870 and the End of Reconstruction in Florida," pp. 360-61.

rejection of returns made by precinct inspectors, or by county canvassers, on the grounds of informality."[30]

In response to his opponent's charges, Walls laid his case before the House committee on elections. In specifications concerned with Duval, Columbia, Jackson, and Gadsden counties, he charged that illegal voting, fraud, and intimidation of his supporters had resulted in the loss of several hundred votes. According to him, there had also been illegal preparation of the ballot boxes in Manatee County, more votes cast than voters registered in Suwannee County, and some returns sent to Niblack before they were forwarded to the state board. Walls insisted there had been the requisite number of signatures on the Alachua County returns, proof of which lay in the county clerk's office, while the Escambia board of canvassers had already rejected the navy yard returns. Those votes had not been included in the official total at all. Walls declared that upon "a fair, legal, and full canvass, he was the winner by 2,785 votes."[31]

The rules for deciding contested elections in the House of Representatives were explicit as to the time allotted for taking depositions, gathering other forms of evidence, and presenting the case. Each party had to notify his opponent prior to any legal maneuvering. In doing so, both the nature of the evidence to be collected and the names of the witnesses called had to be included. These rules were observed strictly in all such cases before the House committee, a fact which tended to expand the time between filing briefs and final decisions. Niblack tried to inform Walls that testimony would be taken beginning on February 27, 1871, in Tallahassee, Jacksonville, and Lake City, and that he intended to examine also the three state officials in charge of the election. Walls, however, never received this notice, which had been left at his old address in Newnansville on February 16. On December 26, 1870, he and Ella had moved to Gainesville from their farm three miles outside Newnansville. He had left Florida on February 14, arriving in Washington three days later, and had taken his seat in the House of Representatives on March 4. He had secured lodging on F Street, within easy walking distance of the capitol. Walls first learned that his election was to be contested in a letter from Florida secretary of state Jonathan Gibbs on April 8. Gibbs informed him that Niblack had issued subpoenas to the state election officials. As a result Walls asked for, and received, a time extension to gather his own evidence as to the "allegations of violence and

30. United States Congress, 42d Cong., 2d sess., *House Miscellaneous Document 34*, "Papers in the Case: Niblack."
31. Ibid., "Papers in the Case: Walls."

fraud." This plea for delay was dated January 31, 1872,[32] which meant the contest had been open at least eleven months. The only possible explanation for the time lapse is the fact that the committee had twelve other cases to adjudicate in the Forty-second Congress. Another full year would pass before the outcome was finally decided.

In the meantime each man continued to gather evidence. Most of Niblack's witnesses were precinct and county election officials who swore that no fraudulent procedures had been utilized to keep Negroes from voting. Generally, these officials pointed out that the polling lines were unusually long, a result of the interest generated by the campaign. Moreover, they charged that Negroes had arrived at the polls armed and looking for trouble. William Paschall, an election inspector in Lake City, testified that Negroes "were allowed all the privileges that the whites were, and the whites gave way to let the colored have their turn at voting, except early in the morning, when there was a great crowd, and the colored people seemed loath to crowd in." To relieve the pressure, Paschall said he opened a door, posted a guard, and admitted many blacks inside to vote.[33]

At Lake City, there was some violence. As Walls was contending here, as elsewhere, that these incidents had prevented large numbers of Negroes from voting, Niblack offered testimony to the contrary. Joseph Tolbert, a resident of Columbia County, described the affair: "The next thing that attracted my attention was a noise on the plank-walk up the street. . . . I found it was a column of colored men, in double file, marching down the plank-walk. There I saw a great many more guns in the hands of those colored men. . . . About that time, a little further up the plank-walk, I heard some pretty rough language being used by some of the parties. I went immediately to the place to keep down a fuss, if possible. . . . I saw a colored man draw his gun. . . . He and a white man, it seems, were in dispute. I stepped up to the white man and put my hand on his shoulder, and endeavored in the name of the State to command the peace. The colored man then turned his gun and took it by the muzzle and struck twice at the white man, the breech of the gun hitting the plank-walk. . . . About that time another white man caught this man, upon whom I had my hand, around the waist . . . and one or two colored men caught this colored man who had struck him with his gun, and kept him from making further demonstrations." Tolbert went on to describe

32. Application for Time Extension, Contested Election of Silas L. Niblack versus Josiah Walls. The Gibbs letter to Walls has not been preserved.
33. *House Document 34*, "Evidence of Contestant," p. 23.

how the Negroes returned to the scene, "making threats that they would burn the town to ashes." Shots were fired before a truce could be arranged ending the disturbance.[34] Other Niblack witnesses swore Negroes were ordered by certain Republican candidates to bring weapons into the polling areas.

The other side of the issue was described by Hugh Watson, a black resident of Columbia County. Watson testified that on the eve of the election he and a small group of Negroes were stopped about a mile from town by six white men "waving their pistols over their heads and cussing us as damn radicals." Later that same evening the black people, after a meeting at the Lake City schoolhouse, started for the center of town: "About this time, we colored were walking two-deep, on the plank-walk. I was one in the front rank when we met these men on the sidewalk, and they were standing two-deep. . . . One pushed me off the sidewalk, and pushed along side the head with his pistol. Then we stepped aside and gave them the plank-walk, and came up the street. After we had passed them they followed us up. After we had gone a right smart piece we stopped and turned up another street. This party still followed us. We again stopped, and they retreated and went back to the sidewalk. We then turned back, passed by them, and went back toward the school-house. After we had passed them a short distance, we were fired into from behind." Watson also revealed that the next morning, election day, many blacks decided to return to their homes without voting after Republican state senator E. G. Johnson was prevented from casting his ballot.[35]

Similar testimony was presented in the case of Marianna in Jackson County. The official count indicated that Walls had been elected by a margin of 4 votes, 878 to 874. However, Walls charged he had lost another 400 votes through violence and intimidation. In a clever legal twist, Niblack stated he would not contest Walls' specification to reject the Jackson County returns because the Republican had received the majority of votes. Walls countered by clarification; he argued before the committee that his specification dealing with Jackson County should not be construed as a request for rejection of all the returns. Rather, he asked for the rejection of only such votes as had been "illegally or improperly cast, or concerning which fraud can be clearly proven."[36] As might be expected, the contestant objected to the inclusion of any testimony

34. Ibid., p. 29.
35. Ibid., "Evidence of Sitting Member," p. 99.
36. Ibid., p. 39.

dealing with Jackson County, but his objection was overruled and the evidence Walls gathered in his own defense was admitted.

In answer to a question as to whether there had been a disturbance in Marianna on November 8, Jesse Robinson, the black Jackson County candidate for the legislature, recounted how one Dr. Alexander S. Tennell had struck him while Robinson was approaching the polls. While hitting the black man, Tennell was heard muttering, "Forty acres of land, God damn you, without a mule." Robinson testified that Tennell had kicked him also, while a short distance away, his brother Jerry Robinson was fighting with J. P. Coker, the head of the Klan in Marianna. Coker had pulled a gun and threatened to shoot. Robinson added that some 150 to 200 black would-be voters left the polling areas following the fracas. John Clemons swore that he overheard Coker say to others standing nearby as Robinson approached: "There is a delegate now that comes by here. He may watch me, God damn him, him and all the rest of them." Richard Pooser testified to the fact that the polls closed for more than half an hour during the incident. Several others swore that Judge Anderson, an election official in Jackson County, ordered all the polls closed well before sundown, the time required by state law. Daniel Kemp, an illiterate black man, testified that the polls were shut down at 4:00 P.M. Niblack countered this testimony by illustrating that Kemp was unable to tell time; Kemp replied, however, that he had asked a friend the time at which Anderson had closed the polls. Other Negroes testified that they had been unable even to reach the polls in Marianna because of the violence encountered en route. According to Lewis Glover, his party of some thirty men was stopped at Long's Bottom, four miles from Marianna, by a large band of armed, disguised men. When they refused to turn around, the Negroes were fired upon and scattered in the confusion; most returned to their homes. Either the terrorists were inclined only toward intimidation, or else they were very poor shots, for no one was killed or wounded.[37]

Jonathan Gibbs, secretary of state and a member of the state board of canvassers, testified to the violence he had encountered in Jackson County earlier in the year, but could add nothing concrete concerning election-day violence. However, he did explain the board's reasoning in rejecting several returns on technical grounds. Some of the returns, he said, had not been sent directly to the board, while others had every appearance of having been unsealed before their delivery. In particular, the secretary pointed to the returns from Manatee County. These had

37. Ibid., pp. 40, 44, 47, 49, 52–53.

been forwarded by W. H. Pearce of Polk County, who swore that he had received them by courier from Manatee along with a telegram requesting him to open the contents and send the results to Niblack in Lake City. This Pearce did, which also explains how the Conservative candidate could begin to ready himself for a contested election case prior to the official publication of results. Gibbs also distinguished between intimidation and the Conservative threats made to prevent radical frauds. He frankly expressed his opinion that the Conservatives wanted to maintain the spirit of violence and fear among Negroes in Florida. Under further cross-examination, he also denied that board member Sherman Conant had ever stated that in fact Bloxham and Niblack were the true winners of the election.[38]

Walls produced testimony confirming voter intimidation in Gadsden County. Marcellus Stearns, county election inspector, testified that several Conservatives who had voted earlier in the day took over one of the three polls in Quincy to prevent its use by Negroes. He claimed that some 200 black Republicans were kept away from the polls, that when they tried to cast ballots, they were refused. According to Stearns, no Democrat was similarly denied.[39] A county election supervisor, A. M. Harris, informed black would-be voters that their names were not on the registration lists. In all, Walls called twenty-nine witnesses who swore that if they could have voted, they would have supported the Republican ticket.

Niblack's retort to the evidence amassed by Walls in proof of violence and intimidation rested on an ingenious interpretation of law:

> Certainly it is dangerous to assume that he who is defeated may yet be declared elected, because somebody, somewhere, did something, said something, or intended something, which frightened some other persons from voting. And the absurdity is increased when . . . we are asked to assume that the color of [the] frightened may determine how [they] would have voted.
>
> There is nothing in the laws of Florida which gives any right to the State Canvassers to exclude votes because of intimidation or violence. . . . [The] House Committee on Elections, however, decided in the case of Giddings vs. Clark that Texas law allowed such a right. The law of Florida being silent on the question . . . the naked question is, whether or not, fugitive and contradictory statements of witnesses can be received, not to prove known facts,

38. Ibid., p. 61.
39. Ibid., p. 74.

but supposed probabilities, not to defeat the vote of the supposed disorderly precinct, but to superadd to the sitting member's majority. Certainly this principle can not be tolerated.[40]

The House Committee did manage to tolerate the principle of adding votes to a majority. Their decision to add twenty-nine votes to Walls' total in Gadsden County rested not only on case-law precedent, but also on the concept that the sitting member's majority was not clearly established while an election was being contested. Moreover, concrete proof of voter-proscription in Gadsden County was based upon the indictment, conviction, and sentence handed to ex-governor Abraham K. Allison in the United States District Court, northern district of Florida, on February 12, 1872, for "obstructing, delaying, and preventing citizens from voting."[41]

Neither party gathered much evidence concerning the Duval County returns. However, W. A. McLean, Duval County court judge and a member of the board of county canvassers, cited clear examples of fraudulent procedures in several county precincts. The judge testified that the returns from the Baldwin area, showing the totals for each candidate in numerals rather than written out, revealed that Walls' fourteen votes had been altered to four. Also, the county judge's office had received no returns at all from Mayport. With respect to the Yellow Bluff precinct, McLean stated that on November 11, George Calder, a precinct canvasser, handed him a sealed envelope upon the request of unknown persons. McLean opened the envelope and found it to contain purported returns from Yellow Bluff. However, Calder unequivocally affirmed these were not official tallies, and that the true number of votes for Niblack at Yellow Bluff was 164, not 383 as the suspicious count indicated. As a result, the county canvassers concluded that the returns from Yellow Bluff had been suppressed; therefore, these votes were excluded from the official certificate.[42]

F. A. Dockray, the county election official who had administered the oaths of office to the precinct inspectors at Yellow Bluff, testified under oath that he had heard the official result of the voting at Yellow Bluff as 164. Of the three precinct inspectors involved, Calder, Isadore Van Balsan, and R. Tombs, the culprit apparently was Van Balsan. He was

40. George W. Paschall, *Contested Election. Silas L. Niblack vs. Josiah T. Walls, from Florida. Argument for Contestant*, p. 9.
41. Exhibit B, *House Document 34*, "Evidence of Sitting Member," p. 75.
42. Ibid., "Evidence of Contestant," p. 6; "Evidence of Sitting Member," p. 110.

tried and convicted in the United States District Court, northern district of Florida, on April 5, 1872, for "concealing, withholding, and destroying election certificates."[43] Dockray was also tried in the case, but freed. It has been suggested that both Dockray and Van Balsan were culpable, but that Van Balsan was tried by a jury bound under the Iron-Clad Oath, denying former rebels the right to sit in judgment without fear of perjury, while the Dockray case was not so tried.[44]

Under friendly questioning by Alva A. Knight, one of Walls' attorneys, Sherman Conant, who had replaced A. R. Meek as attorney general, amplified Gibbs' testimony as to why the state board rejected returns from several election districts. According to Conant, many of the returns were not received in the required length of time; others were defective in manner and form, while still others were kept back because they had been altered. Conant had sent Harry E. Russell of Ocala to Sumter, Hernando, Manatee, and Polk counties to find out why their returns had not been made public. Russell started out from Tampa but was accosted by an armed group of Conservatives who informed him they knew the reason for his journey. He was warned to leave that section of Florida if he valued his life. Conant further testified that "in some of the largest colored counties in the State hundreds of voters had been kept away from the polls by intimidation and violence—by hell raised in general."[45]

It fell to the House committee on contested elections to sift the evidence and to decide two things—who was the legitimate representative of the voters of Florida, and what was the actual margin of victory. As contestee, Walls was more interested in the latter; to offset a possible loss of votes, he rested his defense upon the principle that, potentially, his actual margin of victory could have been much higher. It had been the Conservative resort to violence, intimidation, and fraud which reduced the Republican turnout. Niblack, on the other hand, established four specific points of law and interpretation to support his case. First, he argued that no violent incidents had occurred in most places to intimidate Negroes or prevent their voting. Second, in those few instances where some clashes had taken place, the Negroes were at fault. Third, the state board of canvassers had no discretionary power to reject votes on hearsay evidence. Their function was administrative—to count, record, and publish the official total of all votes cast in an election. Fourth,

43. Ibid., "Evidence of Sitting Member," pp. 111, 113–14.
44. Ralph L. Peek, "Curbing of Voter Intimidation in Florida," p. 335.
45. *House Document 34*, "Evidence of Sitting Member," p. 115.

the Constitution and the state of Florida guaranteed that the civil rights of all citizens included the right to have their votes counted in any election.[46]

The committee decided in Niblack's favor on January 29, 1873, two years after the case had opened. The readjusted totals showed a 137-vote margin, 12,397 to 12,260.[47] The committee did not find satisfactory evidence of fraud and intimidation in Lake City. In Gadsden County, they concluded there had been "an organized effort" by Conservatives to prevent a full vote from being cast. To counteract the proscription of votes, the contestee was awarded an extra 29 votes, equaling the number of witnesses Walls had called. However, this was four fewer than he claimed in his original specification. Walls gained nothing from Jackson County, although he charged that violence and intimidation there had prevented 400 Republicans from voting. The House committee reversed the state board of canvassers by counting two Lafayette County precincts left out in the official results, and at the same time throwing out 42 Walls votes from New Troy as "tainted with fraud." The committee also let stand as recorded the returns from Suwannee, Calhoun, Sumter, Monroe, and Taylor counties. This action came after Niblack waived certain technical objections to some precinct counts; overall, the vote in all but Monroe County had been in his favor. The critical hinge was Duval County, where the heavy Conservative vote had been set aside. The House committee accepted these returns, despite the evidence of fraud; as a result, Walls was unseated.[48] On that same day, January 29, 1873, Niblack was sworn into office.

In Florida there was little surprise at the announcement of the decision, even among the state's Republican newspapers. The *Jacksonville Weekly Republican* noted the case had been settled "in accordance with the facts and the right. Both men will no doubt be paid for the full term, and all because the wrong man, through political influences, was given the certificate of election."[49] The Conservative Tallahassee newspaper wryly observed that Niblack's victory would be short lived as he was to go out of office in less than two months.[50]

46. Paschall, *Contested Election*, pp. 9–10.
47. United States Congress, 42d Cong., 2d sess., *House Miscellaneous Document 52*, pp. 101–6; *Congressional Globe*, 42d Cong., 3d sess., pp. 949–52.
48. *Congressional Globe*, 42d Cong., 3d sess., pp. 949–52. There was also a minority report filed by Congressman Arthur of Kentucky which, although also finding for Niblack, resulted in a slightly different final vote; see appendix, *Congressional Globe*, 42d Congress.
49. February 5, 1873.
50. (Tallahassee) *Weekly Floridian*, January 21, 1873.

Even before this dispute was settled, the two men had faced each other again in the 1872 campaign. By this time, politics had become even more complex than in the past, both in Florida and in the rest of the nation. The national Republican party had splintered with the establishment of the Liberal Republican movement. Dissidents in the party attacked the excesses of the Grant administration and opposed his renomination for a second term. In the state, there were now two congressional seats open for election as well as the senate seat of Thomas Osborn. Florida Republicans, those of the regular faction, met in early August 1872 to select their candidates for the available positions. Walls and William Purman, the nominee from the first congressional district (western Florida), were both chosen by acclamation on the second day of the convention in Tallahassee.

However, political fireworks exploded upon the nomination of Harrison Reed for the United States Senate by Hillsborough County Judge James T. Magbee. At that point Walls burst down the aisle, came forward, and "in a very excited and determined manner," renounced the nomination he had been awarded. Reed had decided to try for the senate seat without the black support which had sustained him as governor. Osborn, however, was renominated, and Walls apologized publicly for his outburst and retracted his statement of withdrawal.[51] At this convention also, Ossian B. Hart was nominated for governor and Marcellus Stearns was chosen as his running mate.

One cause of the split within Republican ranks in Florida during this period was the continuing dissatisfaction of the former southern unionists. On March 15, 1872, William Eaton Chandler, member of the national Republican executive committee, received a letter from R. W. Healy, a native southerner, who explained why the Republican position in Florida was so precarious. Healy argued that "however great their Republicanism, Patriotism, or love for the Union, it is almost impossible to persuade a 'native' to vote for a negro, and with difficulty, for any person who did not come here with the Indians."[52] He predicted that unless southern unionists gained more power within the regular ranks, they and the Conservatives would combine against the carpetbaggers and blacks.

This was the coalition that comprised Liberal Republican–Democratic successes elsewhere. In Missouri, for example, B. Gratz Brown had won

51. *Tallahassee Sentinel*, August 10, 1872.
52. R. W. Healy to William Chandler, March 15, 1872, William Eaton Chandler Papers, vol. 20.

the governor's race against a regular Republican opponent; the Democrats had offered no candidate, choosing to support Brown instead.[53] The Florida Democratic party, led by William Bloxham, was hopeful that a similar maneuver could be engineered in its home state. Bloxham even urged that black delegates be admitted to the Conservative nominating convention because "there will be a liberal Republican convention in session at the same time whose cooperation and support we want."[54] In the Conservative nominating convention, Niblack again won the bid to challenge Walls.

Republican factionalism continued unabated in the campaign. Disconsolate over his loss of a possible senate seat, Harrison Reed approached both Chandler and President Grant. Reed wanted to remove Sherman Conant and Horatio Bisbee, Jr., from their posts as federal marshal and district attorney, contending both men were conspiring with Conservative ex-governor David S. Walker to overthrow the Republican party. According to Reed, if Grant did not remove them from office, he would lose Florida's four electoral votes by a 5,000-vote margin.[55] Republicans all over the state were angered at Reed's attempt to wrest control of Florida Republican politics. Walls and Alva Knight left for Washington and a conference with Grant on October 7, 1872. Others joined in appealing the removal. Bisbee turned to Henry S. Sanford, career diplomat and Florida entrepreneur, to implore that influential figure to exert his prestige with Washington to thwart Reed. Bisbee asserted that Osborn had become weak, and neither he nor Conant could continue to support him for senator.[56] By mid-October, the muddle had cleared. Through the efforts of Walls, Knight, Sanford, and other Republicans, Conant and Bisbee were reinstated by Grant on October 11. Realizing his own defeat, Reed reconciled himself with his fellow Republicans and decided to stump the state in behalf of the party nominees.[57]

The Liberal splinter group, meanwhile, had met earlier in conjunction with the Conservatives. Both conventions were held in Jacksonville on August 14. However, the Conservative party decided to ignore the

53. William E. Parrish, *Missouri under Radical Rule, 1865–1870*, p. 310.

54. William Bloxham to Robert Davidson, July 30, 1872.

55. Harrison Reed to Senator Henry Wilson, quoted in (Tallahassee) *Weekly Floridian*, October 8, 1872.

56. Horatio Bisbee to Henry S. Sanford, October 9, 1872, Henry Shelton Sanford Papers. Sanford was Lincoln's first diplomatic appointment, as minister to Belgium, and a close friend of Grant.

57. Edward M. Cheney to Chandler, October 11, 1872, Chandler Papers, vol. 33.

dissenters beyond token recognition. The Democrats nominated only candidates from their own party for the available slots and, as a result, many of the Liberal Republicans returned to the regular fold. Those who did not return joined the Conservatives "in an absolute surrender."[58] Even as early as July, Osborn had observed that "the Greeley feeling is weaker here than in any other state."[59]

The campaign was underway in earnest by September. Basking in their new-found unity, many Republicans were optimistic about their political future. Alva A. Knight reported that "Florida is safe for Grant and Wilson. Hon. O. B. Hart and Major M. L. Stearns are working the situation in South Florida and are meeting with great success." Knight and Walls were busy traveling the campaign circuit, which included "large and enthusiastic meetings" at Lake City, Madison, Monticello, and Tallahassee.[60] In the capital city Walls made a lengthy speech criticizing Bloxham and Greeley. He dismissed the dissension among Leon County Republicans by stating: "It makes no difference to us whom you support for the State Senate so long as he is a Republican. But we do want your vote for every man on the State Ticket." Walls also observed that some of his race had promised to vote for Bloxham. "In doing so," he said, "they put me in mind of the colored man up North who had promised a white man he would vote a certain way. On the day of the election he was found with another ticket other than the one he had promised to vote. On being asked what it meant he said: 'Massa John, that was talk the other day; this is business.' And so I am confident," Walls continued, "that any promises that Bloxham has received is only talk, and on the fifth of November, you will show him you mean business." On the subject of Greeley or Grant, Walls maintained that the former "has no more claims on you than any other Democrat," while Grant, on the other hand, "has always expressed himself in favor of equal privileges to all." He concluded his speech by describing a Bloxham victory, even if Bloxham himself were to switch parties, as "at most a Republican head and a Democratic body."[61]

The issue of Walls' birth made another appearance during the campaign. However, this time he affirmed rather than denied that he had

58. Thomas Osborn to Chandler, July 11, 1872, ibid., vol. 24.
59. Osborn to Chandler, August 17, 1872, ibid., vol. 27.
60. Alva A. Knight to Chandler, September 15, 1872, ibid., vol. 30.
61. *Tallahassee Sentinel*, September 21, 1872. The black dilemma concerning the Liberal and stalwart split will be discussed more fully in a later chapter. Let it suffice here to note that Walls' allegiance to Grant and the regular party wing was called into question by the national executive committee.

been born a slave. The week after the Tallahassee rally, Walls and Wilkinson Call, the Liberal Republican candidate for United States senator, found themselves on the same podium at a Chattahoochee rally. Call attacked Walls, labeling him "incompetent," "unworthy of trust," and nothing better than a "Pennsylvania carpetbagger." In reply Walls pointed to his record in Congress to dismiss the charge of incompetency. As for being a Pennsylvania carpetbagger, Walls suggested that while such a fate would not distress him, it was untrue. As a Virginia slave, he had "never felt the daylight of freedom."[62]

Walls was also forced to consider affairs in Alachua County. Harmon and Leonard Dennis had split the party, and Harmon had announced himself as an independent candidate for the state senate. Walls moved in to support Harmon, his close friend and associate, who was described at this time as "one of the shrewdest colored men in the State . . . of liberal education, a fine and elegant speaker, and anti-ring."[63] At a local meeting of county Republicans on October 22, Dennis, the "Little Giant," had forced Theodore Gass from the regular ticket as a candidate for the assembly because he had declared his support for Harmon. Upon hearing about Dennis' activities, Walls moved in to do battle. He condemned the Dennis-inspired move to dump Gass from the ticket and promised that if the move stood, he would stump the county for an entire week prior to the election in Harmon's behalf and cause "Rome to howl and the mountains to quake."[64] Gass remained on the ticket and Harmon won the election. Dennis was forced to capitulate.

Walls won the November election by a margin of 1,662 votes, and the Conservatives did not contest the outcome. There are at least two reasons why he fared so well in the 1872 campaign. First, the enforcement of legislation against illegal and violent tactics employed in past elections had succeeded by this time in reducing terrorism. As a result, more blacks could safely vote. Then, too, it seemed as if the party at last had come close to resolving, or at least overlooking, its factional differences. During the spring, it appeared that Reed's maverick role in Republican circles and the Liberal Republican movement would spell ruin for the party in Florida. Yet the Republicans had managed a concerted effort to win. However, this unity was not permanent, and by 1874 factionalism again threatened Republican politics.

62. Ibid., September 28, 1872.
63. Sidney T. Bates to Chandler, April 15, 1872, Chandler Papers, vol. 21.
64. (Tallahassee) *Weekly Floridian*, November 5, 1872.

4

Black against White: J. J. Finley and the 1874 Campaign

I N 1874 Josiah Walls began his third congressional campaign. By that time the political situation in Alachua County and in the state had made his renomination difficult, if not impossible. The Republicans were splintered again by many differences, aggravated by the economic discontent of depression times. High taxes, poor crop returns, and declining money values replaced Reconstruction as the critical issue. White and black Republicans moved farther apart. Also, during Walls' absence from Alachua County, "Little Giant" Leonard Dennis had moved to consolidate his own political leadership. Faced with considerable obstacles to continuing his career, Walls came home from Washington at the end of the Forty-third Congress determined to achieve three goals—to reassert his leadership in the county, to augment his personal power and prestige, and to capture renomination to the House of Representatives.

Beginning in 1873, he had set out to enlarge his personal fortune and expand his business affairs. With his congressional earnings Walls purchased a large plantation on April 19, 1873, in Alachua County, bordering on the northern and western side of Alachua Lake (present-day Payne's Prairie). Previously owned by a former Confederate general, James W. Harrison of South Carolina, who had settled there after the war, Harrison's Landing was considered one of the finest cotton-producing plantations in the state. Walls bought 1,175 acres, of which 1,000 acres had been a part of Duncan L. Clinch's famed Lang Syne plantation in Florida's antebellum days.[1] The price was $5,620. There

1. Deed Book I, p. 41, Clerk of the Circuit Court, Alachua County Courthouse. The mortgage on the Lang Syne plantation owned by Clinch described its location on "the westward of the Alachua Savanna, containing three thousand acres." See Clinch Papers.

was little doubt that Walls was qualified to handle the burdens of large-scale farming; even the conservative Tallahassee newspaper predicted that the new owner would "do well with his ventures."[2] Coincidentally, Silas Niblack at this same time was investing money, his back pay from Congress, in a cotton factory. This event prompted the *Live Oak Times* to remark that Walls could make cotton "for the Hon. Silas to spin. 'Thus business is business.' "[3]

Walls also began to practice law. During the spring term of the Alachua circuit court in 1873, he applied for and was granted admission to the Florida bar. He went before an examination committee appointed by the judge of the circuit court. Three Gainesville attorneys, Robert Taylor, George Arnow, local postmaster, and Samuel Y. Finley, former mayor of Gainesville, found him competent in the law and made a favorable recommendation to the court. He was sworn in during the session.[4] Eventually Walls, Henry Harmon, who had been admitted to the bar in 1869, and William U. Saunders, who would be admitted in 1874, joined forces in a Gainesville law firm providing legal services to Alachua County Negroes. Nothing is known of the firm itself, and there are no extant records. Although it is unlikely that many Florida lawyers could have received much formal education for the profession, and Negro lawyers even less, Walls at least had had some prior experience, having served on state legislative committees for judicial reform and parliamentary procedures. He gathered some background in the law as a result of his contest with Niblack. No doubt he added more to his limited but empirical legal knowledge while in Congress.

In September 1873, he embarked on yet another business venture when he purchased the Gainesville *New Era* from General William Birney, now a moderate Republican permanently settled in Gainesville. The paper was intended to counter the *Independent*, owned by Dennis. Walls' paper was the official organ of the fourth judicial circuit, and it had the responsibility of reporting all court proceedings and decisions.

In his initial editorial, September 13, 1873, Walls pointed out that "no more striking demonstration of the peaceable and law abiding character of [Gainesville] . . . can be given . . . than the publication of a paper . . . by one of the newly enfranchised."[5] He promised a new direction: "A

2. (Tallahassee) *Weekly Floridian*, May 5, 1873.
3. Quoted ibid.
4. (Gainesville) *New Era*, quoted ibid., April 22, 1873.
5. Ibid., September 23, 1873. There are no extant copies of the *New Era* from the period when Walls owned it.

leading feature of the paper will be the discussion of internal improvements, and it will favor every legitimate and judicious effort to develop the resources of the county." Quite obviously, the *New Era* under black ownership would emphasize things and news of particular interest to Negroes. In that regard, Walls promised that the "wants and interests of the people of color will receive special attention. The counsel of the wise and good will be gathered for their benefits. Education, temperance, thrift, economy, and industry will be commended. Societies for mutual improvement will be encouraged." Moreover, and equally obvious, the political focus of the *New Era* was to be shifted. Although Birney was a moderate Republican, Walls intended to make the paper even more Republican (i.e., radical) in outlook, that being one of the primary reasons for his purchase of the paper. Using a military metaphor, he described the new politics of the *New Era*: "It is needless to say that the politics of the 'New Era' will be changed. When a fortification is captured its guns are reversed. The 'New Era' will sustain Republican principles and the Republican party. This will be done, however, without bitterness to opponents and with full recognition of the right of every man to think for himself and of the fact that the best men will differ."[6]

Despite professions to the contrary, however, there was much bitterness in Alachua County politics in 1873–74. Walls, Dennis, and Cessna intensified their feuding in many ways throughout this period. Although the protracted struggle had begun with the party's birth, it had been broken by intermittent truces until mid-1873. Now the local factions were completely at odds. Sometime during this period, Walls became the mayor of Gainesville. Neither the exact dates of his term in office nor a record of his administration are available, but a few details are clear. He served in the summer of 1873, resigning on or about September 1. His successor, a pro-Walls white Republican, was Watson Porter, Gainesville postmaster and physician. Porter took over the office after a "quiet election."[7] He was one of Walls' warmest supporters throughout his public career. (They not only shared political bonds, but Porter served under Walls in the Florida state militia and attended him when he became severely ill in the late 1890s.)

Not content with the executive power, less than a month later Walls replaced Henry Harmon on the county board of public instruction. He did this to contest the moderate Dennis faction over an attempted

6. Ibid., October 7, 1873.
7. Ibid., September 9, 1873.

removal of Porter who was also principal of the Gainesville Union Academy at that time. During the first week of November 1873, Dennis and Cessna decided to remove Porter by force and replace him with a man of their own political persuasion. They went to the school to carry out their aim, only to find Walls and his friends at the schoolhouse door. The details are not clear, save for the fact that Porter remained in his office, and that there was no damage beyond "a few hours of interruption of school operations."[8] However, one can imagine that the scene at the Union Academy was a near fistfight, for about a month later one occurred elsewhere. Walls and the pro-Dennis Alachua County treasurer, a black man named Mayo, engaged in a "scrimmage" in the local blacksmith's shop. The encounter was brief and vicious; both men fought with sledges and pieces of scrap iron. Although nearby observers left the shop, Mayo was reported to have come out "second-best."[9]

This intra-Republican dispute entered its critical phase as the time for nominations approached. Walls had yet to demonstrate his hold on the county, much less his ability to carry the second district. The Republican convention was scheduled for Jacksonville on August 11, and both Dennis and Walls were determined to head the Alachua delegation. For Walls there were only two open courses of action: he had either to reach a compromise with his opponents or defeat them in a power play. In confidence or desperation, but with certain resolve, Walls decided upon the latter. In May he caused a split in the county Republican party. He led his so-called New Departure Republicans against the regulars who were under the aegis of the "Little Giant."

The dangers were obvious. His failure to capture control would have meant the end of his political career. Walls was warned by the *Tallahassee Sentinel* not to run the risks of an independent campaign: "If we are not deceived in the man, his patriotism and party fealty would scout the idea of being made instrumental in dividing the Republican party in Alachua, and jeopardizing its interests. Mr. Walls is sagacious enough to know that he or no other man can revolutionize the Republican party in the State; and he also knows that his strength is owing to faithful adherence to party organization. No man is stronger than his party, and he who trifles with it under the vain illusion that he can work outside and independent of its power will soon find himself politically bankrupt."[10]

8. Ibid., November 11, 1873. *The Records of the Board of Public Instruction of Alachua County, Florida* contain a void from 1871 to 1874. Volume 1 begins in 1869, and volume 2 ends in 1877.

9. (Gainesville) *New Era*, October 28, 1873.

10. May 9, 1874.

He did not submit, and the political advice freely given went unheeded. He answered the editorial admonishment, however, by confirming that he, too, opposed party divisions "based on sectional hatred or prejudice to race." He denied any intent to wage an independent campaign:

> I therefore feel it to be an indispensable duty that I owe to the State and the party that I have the honor in part to represent and to the race with which I am identified, to say publicly to the people of Florida, particularly to the colored people . . . that I would sincerely deprecate any movement looking to the division of the people of our fair State, upon sectional hatred or prejudice to race. I have no ambition politically or otherwise that will induce me to misrepresent what I believe to be the true interest of my race, the State I represent, and the interest of the party that has twice elected me to Congress.
>
> Colored men, we have nothing to gain by an issue with the white race, nor has the interest of the State anything to gain by an open political issue between its citizens based on sectional hatred, and in no way will I be a party to such an issue.[11]

Walls was embroiled in a distasteful fight which centered on race. Even though both he and Dennis had biracial support in the county, black and white Republicans were moving farther apart. At the state Republican central committee meeting on July 4, in the United States courthouse in Jacksonville, the party leaders settled on the platform planks and dates for their district conventions. The second district convention was set for the same site, Jacksonville, on August 11. Walls had little more than a month to regain control of Alachua County.

He returned to Gainesville on July 9 and began to work. He called a party executive meeting two days later to select delegates to a county-wide Republican convention on July 25, where the delegation would be ratified for the second district's August 11 nominating convention. Walls "packed" the executive meeting. By wielding his power as chairman, he managed to apportion more delegates from Newnansville than from either Pineville or Pleasant Plains, two larger Alachua County precincts which were both Dennis strongholds.[12]

The county meeting of Alachua Republicans was held at the courthouse in Gainesville on Saturday, July 25. It was a festive occasion; the

11. (Jacksonville) *Tri-Weekly Union*, June 2, 1874; (Tallahassee) *Weekly Floridian*, June 2, 1874. Because of its numerous title changes in this period, hereafter all references to the *Tri-Weekly*, *Weekly*, or *Daily Florida Union* will be cited as *Florida Union*.

12. (Jacksonville) *The New South*, July 15, 29, 1874.

Lone Star Band played patriotic songs to entertain the large crowds which had gathered to listen to the speech-making. On the speaker's stand, Walls faced one of the most crucial moments of his life. When his turn came to address his fellow Republicans he delivered an emotional, two-hour speech. Here again, the full speech has not been preserved, but it is known from newspaper reports that he pursued the regulars with no mercy. Before the biracial crowd, he charged that there were no more than eight white "true" Republicans in Alachua County. No doubt, he also alluded to the political proscription that he and other blacks had suffered at the hands of the moderate leadership.

Then it was the opposition's turn. William Cessna attacked Walls' federal appointments, especially the nomination of William Saunders as a customs official at Cedar Key.[13] Saunders had been originally appointed as assistant customs official at Cedar Key under a man named Blumenthal who had tried to fire Saunders for incompetence. In retaliation Congressman Walls had attempted to replace Blumenthal first with Henry Harmon, and then with Saunders.[14] Cessna produced a letter allegedly written by Walls, urging President Grant to consider his recommendation. Surprised at this move, Walls first denied the authenticity of the letter. When pressed, however, he reversed his stand and acknowledged its authorship. But before Cessna could continue his demolition attack, the Lone Star Band, presumably hired by the executive chairman, drowned out the speaker. According to a reporter covering the scene, Walls and Cessna continued their battle. He described how the two men remained to "altercate, fulminate, deprecate, irritate, and exasperate" each other.[15]

In the end, Walls was successful. The predominantly black pro-Walls crowd ratified the "New Departure" faction. The delegates were not actually voted upon, however; they already had been selected by Walls at the executive meeting. The Alachua delegation to Jacksonville endorsed their leader, pledged themselves in his behalf, and reelected him chairman of the county executive committee.[16] It was a total victory. Neither Dennis nor Cessna was a member of the district delegation, while Henry Harmon and Watson Porter both were chosen.

Walls easily won the bid in Jacksonville. After a first-ballot victory on a 66 to 2 vote, he was nominated by acclamation. His only challenger was

13. (Jacksonville) *Florida Union*, August 6, 1874.
14. Ibid., June 23, 1874.
15. Ibid., August 6, 1874.
16. (Jacksonville) *The New South*, July 29, 1874.

Dennis Eagan, Madison County legislator and member of the state Republican central committee. The two Eagan votes were cast by the Volusia County delegation. The only other anti-Walls sentiment was expressed by United States District Attorney Horatio Bisbee, Jr., of Jacksonville. Bisbee felt that Walls had acted improperly concerning his federal appointments of Saunders and Harmon. Yet he too offered his support.[17] The nominating convention was brief, and an easy win for the candidate. The campaign was neither.

There were several points of contention about Walls during the campaign. In the first place, many people were opposed to a third term for the incumbent. The Republican *Tallahassee Sentinel* opposed his bid for this reason, although it described him as an "able, clear-headed, honest, and unselfish politician, and . . . a statesman of no mean order." The newspaper pointed out that he had received some $24,000 in congressional salary since 1870, plenty enough for one man. "There is not one of the number [of Walls' supporters] . . . who would object to a hack at the same butter."[18] In Jacksonville, the Republican papers differed in their views of the candidate. The *Florida Union* indicted him for incompetence, saying he had neither "the training nor the education, nor the application for mental work" required of a congressman.[19] On the other hand, he received warm support from *The New South*, which lauded him as "always industrious . . . and responsive . . . he has as a Representative been always active and vigilant."[20]

His critics leveled three specific charges—the issue of the attempted appointments of Saunders and Harmon, the appointment of former Governor David Walker's son to West Point (actually the Naval Academy), and his possible connection with corruption in the Archer post office of Alachua County. The criticism of the Saunders appointment stated that Walls patronized his close friends. Cessna's attack was accompanied by another in the *Florida Union*.[21] The implication that he delved in unusually corrupt practices by securing offices for his friends is false when considered in light of the times. Most politicians, black and white, Republican and Democrat, from Grant to Walls, did the same thing. As yet, civil service was unknown.

However, the charge that he violated Republican trust by appointing young Acton Walker to West Point must be examined with care, for this

17. Ibid., August 12, 1874.
18. July 18, 1874.
19. July 7, 1874.
20. July 11, 1874.
21. June 23, 1874.

drew fire from blacks as well as whites. E. D. Ward, a Negro Republican from Jacksonville, complained that Walls was "fishing for Democratic favor" by this appointment.[22] Some historians have interpreted his action in this matter as an attempt to smooth relations between races and parties. Neither explanation is satisfactory. Actually, the congressman had appointed a Gainesville youth named Dogan Stringfellow to the United States Naval Academy in April 1873, but the appointee failed to appear for the entrance examination. Thereupon, Walls suggested Walker for the academy. (Acton Walker was never considered for West Point.) Secretary of the Navy William M. Reynolds acknowledged the appointment by a letter to Walls on September 5, 1873. He added that young Walker's credentials also were recommended by Senator Simon B. Conover. Thus, Walls was not the only Republican involved in the controversial appointment. Furthermore, contemporary and secondary critics alike have failed to note that two years earlier, Walls had succeeded in securing the appointment to West Point of Thomas V. Gibbs, son of the black secretary of state.[23]

The most potentially damaging issue to surface concerned corruption in the Archer post office. The controversy centered upon the removal of postmaster Edward Young, who allegedly had misappropriated public funds for Walls' campaign. Young was promised immunity from prosecution by postal agent J. E. Walker if he would swear that Walls knew about this criminal activity. Young did so by affidavit sworn in Jacksonville on July 17, 1874.[24] Walls countered this move to discredit his campaign by denying complicity. Before the full details of the case became public knowledge, he also swore an affidavit, denying that he knew Young personally, or that he had had anything to do with his appointment. Young later recanted his statement, and no conspiracy was ever proved.[25] The Archer case stemmed in part from an earlier situation

22. (Jacksonville) *Florida Union*, May 30, 1874.

23. (Tallahassee) *Weekly Floridian*, September 20, October 28, 1874; *Tallahassee Sentinel*, September 21, 1872. See William Ward, *List of Cadets Admitted into the United States Military Academy, West Point, N.Y., from Its Origin till September 1, 1886*. Walls appointed Gibbs on May 31, 1871, and he entered the following year. He flunked his midterm examination, and despite appeals from his father, General O. O. Howard, and General John T. Sprague, the academy review board declined to reinstate him. See "Letters and Endorsements, United States Military Academy Records, 1872–1874." Dogan Stringfellow was nominated by Walls for the Naval Academy on April 7, 1873. Stringfellow stated his intention to appear for the examination on June 5, but failed to do so. See Naval Academy Records, Register no. 2281.

24. (Jacksonville) *The New South*, July 25, 1874.

25. (Gainesville) *New Era*, quoted in (Tallahassee) *Weekly Floridian*, August 4, 1874. With his recantation, Young lost his immunity from prosecution. Two years later, on May

in the Jacksonville post office. Edward M. Cheney, postmaster and editor of the *Florida Union*, was charged with swindling the Freedmen's Bank in Jacksonville. The charge had been made by a mail order clerk, and upon the recommendation of the entire Florida congressional delegation, Cheney was removed from office. J. E. Walker, incensed by the removal of his close friend, retaliated by incriminating Young and Walls.[26] According to William Purman, congressman from the first district, it was this chain of events that accounted for the *Florida Union*'s and Cheney's "intense opposition" to the incumbent.[27] Jacksonville's pro-Walls *The New South* placed Cheney's malice even further back in time. According to that paper, the 1870 post-election investigations into the Yellow Bluff precinct, which had led to several indictments of Cheney's friends, had made the editor a "particular and personal enemy who omitted no opportunity to do [Walls] injury."[28] His attacks were not unanswered by the candidate. He lightly responded by thanking the *Florida Union* for its "gratuitous advertisement" of the Walls, Saunders, and Harmon law firm. The firm pledged that it would not discriminate "on account of race, color, or previous condition, except to editors."[29]

Negroes were themselves divided in their support of Walls in the second electoral district. For a brief period of time two black politicians, John R. Scott and J. Willis Menard, made plans to run against Walls. Scott, who represented Duval County in the state legislature, and Menard, who later became a newspaper editor in Key West, were disaffected with, or jealous of, the incumbent. According to E. D. Ward, their goal was "to lay Mr. Walls on the shelf and bring out a better man this fall." Ward noted that he "has made speeches enough, but done no good. We like more work and less second-hand gas."[30] Walls foiled this effort by publishing the dissenters' plans before they had been fully formulated. Embarrassed by the disclosure, the two men withdrew. At a Gainesville rally in June, Menard attacked Walls for his "unkind cut" in making confidential plans public.[31]

4, 1876, proceedings were begun, charging Young with having embezzled $3,630.32 in money orders from the Archer post office. He was found guilty on December 19. The debt was never paid, and on November 28, 1892, the United States Post Office closed the books by "Bad Debts." Suits against Defaulting Postmasters, Contractors, and Others, for Debts Due the Post Office Department: *United States vs. Edward L. Young and his Sureties*.

26. (Tallahassee) *Weekly Floridian*, July 28, 1874.
27. *The Watchman's Letter*, No. 2, May 20, 1876.
28. July 25, 1874.
29. (Jacksonville) *Florida Union*, June 30, 1874.
30. Ibid., May 30, 1874.
31. (Tallahassee) *Weekly Floridian*, June 23, 1874.

Eventually, Negroes in East Florida coalesced in support of Walls. He was accused of establishing a "black wing" of the Republican party. A public notice was distributed in Alachua and Marion counties, allegedly penned by the candidate, announcing the formation of an independent black party to wage the campaign along racial lines. Walls vehemently denied the charge and authorship of the "Alachua Circular."[32] As the election itself drew near, his support grew. Scott, abandoning his opposition, denounced the *Florida Union* for its nonsupport of the Republican candidate because of "prejudices of race."[33] A Palatka Republican replied to E. D. Ward's criticisms and comments by condemning those who "talk and write as if they carried the colored voters like a pack of cards to be shuffled, dealt, and played at their pleasure."[34] From Mandarin, one William Chase described the candidate as "a distinguished and active delegate, with fine talents." He acknowledged his past opposition to Walls, but now could see no reason why he should not be returned to Congress.[35]

On the other hand, attacks on the candidate also grew. In a derisive tone, the *Florida Union* described the travel arrangements made for the Alachua delegation following the close of the nominating convention. Concerning the trip back to Gainesville, Cheney wrote: "I am informed . . . [that] Walls presented his delegation from Alachua County with railroad tickets to pass them. . . . To Dr. Watson Porter (white) and to (the unsullied) Harmon he gives first-class tickets and to the rest of the colored delegates second-class. Here was only partial civil rights on public conveyances . . . for Harmon is almost white. He carries a cane, parts his hair in the middle, wears a gold watch chain, and is the Beau Brummel of the Alachua delegation."[36]

Negrophobia increased. Sherman Conant, a United States marshal, was castigated for deputizing blacks as election marshals to prevent violence at the polls: "it betokens a recklessness which is almost beyond belief."[37] In the same vein, the *Tallahassee Weekly Floridian* described the Alachua County campaign tactics of Saunders and Harmon, both commissioned by Conant, under the editorial headline "Reign of Terror."

32. (Jacksonville) *Florida Union*, October 8, 1874.
33. John R. Scott to editors, (Jacksonville) *Florida Union*, September 23, 1874, quoted in (Jacksonville) *The New South*, September 26, 1874.
34. (Jacksonville) *Florida Union*, June 2, 1874.
35. Ibid., June 9, 1874.
36. Ibid., August 13, 1874.
37. Ibid., November 21, 1874.

The article portrayed the ruthless tactics these villains reputedly had utilized to deny the right to vote to whites.[38]

Walls' opponent in the 1874 campaign was Jesse J. Finley, another of the antebellum Whigs-turned-Reconstruction-Conservative. Born in Wilson County, Tennessee, in 1814, Finley had migrated to Florida and established a law practice in Marianna by 1846. During the 1850s he had served two terms as judge of the western judicial circuit, and was then appointed as judge of the Confederate district court of Florida in 1861. He resigned his position for military service. He was elected colonel of the Sixth Florida Regiment and was promoted to brigadier general after Chickamauga. At war's end, he returned to Marianna and resumed his law practice before moving to Lake City and then Jacksonville.[39] His credentials were typical for a Conservative candidate in this period. There was another man in the race, W. R. Anno, an independent white supremacist from Jacksonville, who based his campaign upon a non-partisan overthrow of the Negro officeholders. But his campaign received little support, and he soon dropped out.[40]

By this time, some Conservatives had begun to question the continued use of the term "Conservative" instead of "Democrat" with respect to party labels. The emotional connections to slavery, secession, and the war had eased. Moreover, there was no national organization by that name. Some men, such as David Levy Yulee, believed the traditional label would now generate more votes. Prior to either nominating convention, he had written: "The difficulty about an effective campaign in the State . . . is that there is no party. The Democratic party . . . seems to have been put aside. . . . The term 'conservative' conveys no meaning, has no history, no sympathetic party outside, and is in its essentially weak [condition] because it is based upon a sort of deprecation of Republican power in the State and a solicitation of Republicans to join. It is a confession of weakness and a deference to the Republican organization that strengthens them."[41]

Because neither Walls nor Finley engaged in crude verbal exchanges, the campaign in East Florida passed in relative quiet. The issues were not complex, and the voters were divided along racial lines more than anything else. As a result, there were fewer minds open to persuasion by campaign oratory. The real conflict occurred in print, between two

38. N.d., cited ibid.

39. Ibid., September 22, 1874.

40. (Jacksonville) *The New South*, August 15, 1874.

41. David Levy Yulee to unknown, July 20, 1874, David Levy Yulee Papers, mss. box 9.

Jacksonville Republican newspapers, the *Florida Union* and *The New South*. The former had refused to endorse Walls even after the nominating convention, supporting Finley instead. One observer described the campaign and the newspaper conflict in some detail:

> The campaign . . . has been conducted in a very quiet manner, but there has been much good done. I am informed by parties from different parts of the state that the chances for [Finley's] election . . . are very good. While it was thought and so expressed by a good many of our prominent citizens that Genl. Finley was not the most available man that could have been brought out in this District, yet most of the delegates preferred to be defeated under him than to put forward another man whom they did not have so much confidence in. The Genl. is liberal in his views, treats the opposition with courtesy, does not deal in so much of this personal abuse that is getting so common nowadays. It is thought that he will get the vote of all the respectable [white] Republicans in the District. Many of them have already committed themselves, and the "Union" comes out boldly in his favor. It can not swallow Walls. . . . [Sawyer][42] says Walls is incompetent, and that as long as he has any connection with that paper, he will not advocate any man for office whom he thinks is incompetent. If his own party won't nominate good men, he will support the conservative candidates.
>
> On the other hand the "New South" which started out with the promise of being a non-political paper devoted to the interest of the State and the community, ignoring parties &c—has turned out to be the most bitter Radical sheet there is in the State. One would hardly imagine there could be such a change in so short a time. It is as rabbid [*sic*] a Radical sheet as can be found most anywhere.[43]

Republican splintering hurt Walls' chances. In the past, the various factions had managed to arrange a temporary truce to cooperate in the elections. But now, for example, there were two Republican slates of candidates in Duval County. This kind of factionalism worked against Walls. His situation further declined as a result of a debilitating attack of hemorrhoids which left him bedridden for most of July. He had never

42. Sawyer became the editor of the *Florida Union* in 1874 before buying out *The South* and beginning the (Jacksonville)*Tri-Weekly Sun*. See *Tri-Weekly Sun*, January 25, 1876. He also was friendly with several prominent East Florida Conservatives. See Samuel Swann to N. A. Sawyer, n.d., 1875, Samuel Swann Papers.

43. A. Manin to L'Engle, October 30, 1874, mss. box 4, folder 77, Edward L'Engle Papers.

fully recovered from this war-connected illness.[44] The election on November 3, 1874, promised to be close. The results, verified by the state board of canvassers, showed Walls' margin of victory to be only 371 votes, 8,549 to 8,178.[45] On January 7, 1875, J. J. Finley served notice that he would contest the results.[46]

There was one major difference between this and the previous contested election case. Earlier, Niblack and Walls had charged and countercharged violence and intimidation during their race. That case had been decided largely upon the numbers of voters who had or had not been denied the right to vote by fear and threats. In this contest, only one charge of voter intimidation was cited, and that was specified by the Conservative Finley. Moreover, only one charge of conspiracy was noted; that, too, was by the contestant.

Most of the data, testimony, and evidence centered on procedural matters. The contestee, Walls, received the notice of his opponent in Jacksonville on February 3; he made a lengthy reply three days later.[47] Although there were seventeen specifications, it is unnecessary to examine each in detail. However, there were three issues in particular that decided the outcome of the case. These were the matter of oaths, the activity of Saunders at the Archer precinct, and possible fraud at Lake City's Colored Academy precinct in Columbia County.

According to Finley, the state election officials had counted improperly cast votes of several Alachua County precincts, including Archer, Newnansville, Micanopy, Liberty Hill, Gordon, Orange Creek, and Barnes' Store. The crucial factor, apart from Archer, dealt with the oaths administered to the black voters. Under the law in Florida, if any person was challenged at the polls, he was required to swear the following oath, found in section sixteen of the election code: "You do solemnly swear that you are twenty-one years of age; that you are a citizen of the United States (or that you have declared your intention to become a citizen of the United States, according to the acts of Congress on the subject of naturalization); that you have resided in this State one year and in this county six months next preceding this election; that you have not voted at this election, and that you are not disqualified to vote by the judgement of any court."[48]

44. Josiah Walls Pension File.

45. (Tallahassee) Weekly Floridian, December 13, 1874.

46. Ibid., January 8, 1875.

47. "J. J. Finley, contestant, and Josiah T. Walls, contestee, 44th Congress: Answer to notice of contestant" (hereafter cited as "Answer to notice of contestant").

48. U. S. Congress, 44th Cong., 2d sess., House Miscellaneous Document 52, p. 369.

This oath applied only to voters whose names were on the registration lists. If a would-be voter's name were not on the list, he had to swear to another oath (in addition to the above) according to section nine of the election code. That section declared "That if any person whose name may be erased shall, on offering to vote at any election, declare on oath that his name has been improperly struck off from the list of registered voters, and shall take the oath required to be taken by persons whose right to vote shall be challenged," he could then exercise the franchise.[49]

There were two reasons why many voters in the county whose names were not on the lists at the polls did not swear that they had been removed improperly. First, some voters were not double-sworn as the law required because the precinct officials were either unaware of the correct procedure, had no copies of the section nine oath, or administered only rough approximations. M. E. Papy, serving as a precinct inspector in Gainesville, testified that while he had administered an oath, he did not "know if it were the proper oath or not." He added that occasionally he varied the wording, but the substance remained the same. He swore to only honorable intentions to hold a fair election.[50] Second, most voters would not take the section nine oath because they believed their names to be on the master registration lists. The various precincts had only copies from the original lists in the courthouse. Finley charged that all these Alachua County votes were illegal because of the oath violations.

Although the local canvassing agency in fact had rejected these returns, the state board reversed that decision. The House committee on privileges and elections ruled in favor of the local board. It decided that the state election officials performed only a ministerial task in counting the returns. They were not empowered to exercise discretionary judgment as to the legality of the votes cast. Walls contended this interpretation misconstrued Florida's election laws. According to the contestee, the law required all returns to be forwarded to the state board.[51] The House committee disagreed, and then proceeded to determine the vote totals in the county.

The House committee blamed the inspectors, not the voters, for the oath mixups. They concluded that "although the inspectors were at fault in allowing the persons to vote whose names were not on the lists

---

49. Ibid., p. 368.
50. Ibid., p. 373.
51. *Contested Election. Jesse J. Finly* [sic] *v. Josiah T. Walls. Second Congressional District–Florida. Brief for the Contestee*, pp. 1–2 (hereafter cited as *Brief for the Contestee*).

furnished them by the clerk of the circuit court, still, as their names should have appeared on such lists . . . their votes should be counted when their names are found to have been on such registry-lists at the clerk's office."[52] The decision to include most of the votes would seem to have favored Walls. Most of the votes in question were black and Republican; therefore they would have added to his total. However, when the House committee ruled that the state board was to exercise only administrative powers, Walls' totals and lead over Finley were threatened. Because not all the names of questionable voters were found on the registration lists, some votes were purged. All were subtracted from his total.

A more serious charge was contained in the third, fourth, and fifth articles of the contestant's seventh specification concerning the Archer returns:

> 3d. Because at said poll one W. U. Saunders, one of your partisan friends, and partner in the practice of law, claiming to be a deputy United States marshal, under the guise of an assumed authority, illegally dictated to and over-awed the inspectors at said poll, so that they did not, and could not impartially discharge their duties as such officers at said poll:
> 4th. Because a large and excited crowd of your political friends, armed with clubs, &c, so surrounded said poll, so boisterously and violently demeaned themselves, that a number of my supporters left the said poll without voting:
> 5th. Because said W. U. Saunders, a partisan friend to you, and a partner in the practice of law, acting under the color of the authority of a deputy United States marshal, so intimidated and influenced the inspectors at said poll that they yielded the whole control and management of said election to him, supposing that he had the authority; and after said election was over, the said Saunders, by his interference and directions, prevented said inspectors from counting the ballots directed by law, but counted the same himself and sealed up the ballot-box himself without the solicitation of said inspectors.[53]

Testimony was offered by Finley's witnesses that Saunders had stood at the Archer poll during the day of the election "ordering the colored voters into line, [and taking] . . . great interest . . . whenever a Republi-

52. *House Misc. Document 52*, p. 373.
53. "Answer to notice of contestant," pp. 6–7.

can vote was questioned or challenged." Saunders' actions led George C. Helveston, the Conservative election supervisor at the Archer precinct, to feel that he and other election officials had been "intimidated." Green Moore, an election inspector, revealed that a few Conservatives left the poll without voting because of the long lines of blacks. However, he reported that there had been no fighting among those standing around. Green indicated there were "disturbances," referring to the loud talking and occasional arguments around the polling places. The other Archer inspector, William Geiger, stated no actual racial collision had occurred; however, he added one might have been touched off had not the Conservatives left. None of the witnesses indicated any evidence of concealed or brandished weapons. Geiger and Moore also testified that Saunders had assisted in the count, which was repeated several times, and he counted the votes once alone after the clerk had already done so. Geiger, the white inspector, added that Saunders also had helped seal the ballot box at his own request.[54] Acting on this evidence, the House committee concluded that Saunders was guilty of "meddling with the ballots and controlling the order of voting."[55]

The crux of the contested election rested upon allegations of conspiracy and fraud in Lake City at the Colored Academy precinct. There were 588 votes cast for Walls and 11 votes for Finley in this precinct; but in the entire county, Walls received only a 38-vote majority. Thus, when the House committee found a clear intent to commit fraud and rejected the returns from the Colored Academy, the outcome of the case was decided in Finley's favor.

The major indictment in Finley's ninth specification was that Dr. Elisha G. Johnson, the election supervisor at the Colored Academy precinct and a Republican candidate for the Florida state senate, conspired with other election officials to insure a Republican majority. Johnson, precinct election inspectors Charles R. King and John W. Tompkins, precinct clerk Charles R. Carroll, and Duval Selph, a local Republican supporter, were considered equally culpable in the conspiracy. The first charge was that Johnson had opened the precinct poll one hour earlier than prescribed by law. Several witnesses under examination by the contestant testified that the polls had opened at 7:00 A.M. and that at least twenty persons, all black and presumably Republicans, had voted before 8:00 A.M., the proper time. Duval Selph revealed under examination that he had even turned his watch ahead approximately one

54. *Brief for the Contestee*, pp. 39, 42, 43, 44.
55. *House Misc. Document 52*, p. 378.

hour on the eve of the election. The decision to open the poll early was made at Johnson's home on the night of November 2. Selph and Charles King had spent the night there and left early the next morning to open the poll.[56]

A second charge indicative of conspiratorial intent was that none of the men involved, except for Johnson, were duly chosen and authorized election officers. Florida law required that election personnel were to be chosen at the polls from the electorate or by the county commissioners. Finley charged there had been no meeting to accomplish this task and, as a result, Tompkins, King, and Carroll illegally conducted the proceedings at the Colored Academy precinct.

Third, it was charged that Johnson allowed between 75 and 100 persons to vote in an illegal manner. Duval Selph testified that Johnson "called a name and a number and they put it through an aperture in the wall where the ballot-box stood, and called out the name and number, and the ballot was thus received. . . . Johnson called the name and gave the number which he gave to these parties from . . . the registration-list, and the parties took the number with the ticket and passed it through the hole to the inspectors, calling out the name."[57] This illegal procedure enabled many nonresidents of Columbia County to vote under fictitious names. Moreover, it was alleged that at least sixteen persons had voted twice, at the Colored Academy and Market-House precincts. Keightley S. Waldron, clerk of the circuit court of Columbia County, testified he compared the registration lists from both precincts. Waldron never completed his examination of the lists, however; he left the clerk's office on business elsewhere in the county and returned to find his office gutted by fire. The House committee on privileges and elections concluded that "The irregularities at this precinct were not the result of ignorance, inadvertance, or carelessness, but were the result of fraud, and that there were no legally-appointed inspectors, nor a legally-appointed clerk at this precinct; that Johnson took the entire charge of the polls through persons who by his procurement acted as inspectors and clerks. They cannot stand better than mere intruders, having no official character; intruders not for the purpose of aiding in conducting an election fairly, but for the purpose of carrying into execution a previously-arranged fraud upon the ballot-box."[58]

Walls was unable to offer direct evidence in rebuttal as the fire in the

56. Ibid., pp. 383, 385.
57. *Brief for the Contestee*, p. 61.
58. *House Misc. Document 52*, pp. 382–85.

clerk's office had prevented an accurate check of the vote totals. Johnson was murdered by an unknown person or persons on August 13, 1875, and Walls was denied the privilege of taking any testimony in Lake City at all. He had employed counsel to accomplish this for him, but the man had taken ill. The contestee was denied application for a time extension for gathering testimony in the case. The witnesses' recollections were not fresh after the ten-month interval, and the chief principal in the affair was not alive to defend his course of action. Thus, the entire corpus of evidence in the case was ex parte, i.e., only one side.[59]

Despite these handicaps, Walls suggested alternate explanations of what had transpired. First, he raised the question of the opening of the poll. He explained that the time differential between the prescribed and de facto opening of polls, whether longer or shorter, was immaterial if the outcome of the election remained unaffected. Furthermore, his report submitted to the Congress pointed out that the testimony conflicted as to the actual time involved and "among a collection of watches, not probably worth together $10, it would be very unsafe to infer that the voting actually commenced before 8."[60] Whatever the actual time, the more crucial factor was Johnson's supposed intent in opening the polls at an earlier hour. The minority report figured from the 600 votes cast at the Colored Academy precinct that "The polls must open at 8, giving two hundred and forty minutes before 12 o'clock; the sun set November 3 at 4:54, giving two hundred and ninety-four minutes after 12 o'clock. If the poll opened at just 8 am, and closed at sundown, i.e., giving five hundred and thirty-four minutes of time in which to do the work of voting. Now as it was expected to be the place where the colored voters would vote, it was clear that the day must be a diligent one, and a good deal more than one vote must be cast in a minute if the work was to be done. This furnishes an honest and laudable reason why Johnson was in a hurry all day."[61]

A conflicting explanation also was presented concerning the unauthorized election officials. According to John W. Tompkins, the only witness to offer testimony, there indeed had been two constituted officers chosen for the Colored Academy precinct, but they had declined to serve. Johnson was forced to appoint substitutes. Furthermore, "suppose the contestant had shown, as he has not, that these inspectors were neither appointed by the county commissioners nor chosen by the

59. *Congressional Record*, 44th Cong., 1st sess., pp. 2553–55.
60. *Brief for the Contestee*, p. 60; *House Misc. Document 52*, p. 403.
61. *House Misc. Document 52*, pp. 402–3.

electors at the polls; what then? Does he imagine that the acts of de facto officers of an election are less valid than those of de jure officers?"[62]

Because of Johnson's number system, it had been charged that some nonresidents had voted under assumed names, while others had voted twice. Walls replied that these were unprovable allegations. The original registration lists had been destroyed in the fire. Moreover, the whole issue of duplicate and fraudulent votes involved no more than 50 people. He asked why 550 legal voters should be disfranchised.[63] According to section 442 of the *American Law of Elections*, there were two reasons. First, circumstantial evidence was admissible in cases of fraud and conspiracy. Second, in these cases, the whole set of returns could be rejected when the true number of votes was unknown. By a vote of 135 to 84, with 71 abstentions, the House of Representatives unseated Josiah Walls on March 29, 1876.[64]

The report to the House floor was divided, and majority and minority reports were submitted following an 8 to 3 vote on March 9.[65] Even before the final decision, many were convinced that Walls had lost. Sen. Charles W. Jones had predicted the previous October that Finley would win his case.[66] The Washington correspondent to the *Florida Union* reported in early February 1876: "Walls still clings to the ragged edge, but will be let down when the Committee on Privileges and Elections reports. Finley wears his same old smile and is happy, though Walls thinks the smile altogether too winning."[67] Rumors even circulated that William Purman, his colleague from the first district of Florida, worked against the incumbent. In late January the *Florida Union*, never a friend to Walls, charged that Purman desired his defeat to have sole control of federal patronage from the House of Representatives.[68] Purman labeled this "diabolically humorous."[69] After the outcome, Walls returned to Florida on April 24, 1876.[70]

62. *Brief for the Contestee*, pp. 57–58.
63. Ibid.
64. *Congressional Record*, 44th Cong., 1st sess., pp. 2563, 2602.
65. (Jacksonville) *Florida Union*, March 16, 1876.
66. Charles W. Jones to C. C. Yonge, October 6, 1875, C. C. Yonge Papers, mss. box 3.
67. February 17, 1876.
68. (Jacksonville) *Florida Union*, January 31, 1876.
69. *The Watchman's Letter*, No. 1, n.d., quoted in *Tallahassee Sentinel*, January 29, 1876.
70. (Jacksonville) *Florida Union*, April 26, 1876.

5

Race, State, Party, and Self

T HERE is a natural prejudice," Alexis de Tocqueville once observed, "that prompts men to despise whoever has been their inferior long after he has become their equal."[1] Few groups in any historical period have illustrated the truth of de Tocqueville's assessment of human nature more precisely than the black men elected to Congress during Reconstruction. Not only were they scorned by their contemporaries, both inside and out of the Congress, but these Negro politicians, including Josiah Walls, also have been largely ignored by historians. This "white-out" of the black congressmen in Reconstruction has been administered by historians of both races. Samuel Denny Smith's 1940 monograph shares the biases of the "Dunning" historiographic tradition in *The Negro in Congress, 1870–1901*.[2] James Ford Rhodes dismissed their presence entirely by writing of them: "They left no mark on the legislation of their time; none of them, in comparison with their white associates, attained the least distinction."[3] The black historian John Hope Franklin stated that while election to Congress was one of the important ways in which Negroes contributed to politics in Reconstruction, "many bills which they introduced were deemed unworthy of serious consideration. . . . None of the Negro members enjoyed the prestige of being chairman of important committees and had great difficulty in winning the respect

1. *Democracy in America*, 1:357.
2. Smith argued that these black congressmen should have performed ably because of the presence of white blood in their veins. Their failure verified his thesis that it would be better for Negroes to forego politics completely. See pp. 143–44.
3. *History of the United States from the Compromise of 1850*, 7:169–70.

even of colleagues in their own party." Franklin ended this discussion in less than three pages of his seminal work, *From Slavery to Freedom*.[4]

It is not the intention here to argue that Josiah Walls' career diverged from the general historical view of the black congressmen of Reconstruction, nor indeed to suggest they were at all markedly different from what historians have said about them. One thing is clear: Apart from the question of ability, these men were powerless to affect change in a system stacked against them. While politics in this era may have seemed to exhibit a closer sense of association between blacks and whites interacting in new fashion, power remained securely in white hands. Few historians have studied the degree of political awareness, apart from political power, evidenced by black congressmen. In their efforts to appeal to voters of both races and to function effectively as politicians, the congressional leadership group traveled a narrow pathway bordered by the competing interests of their races, their states, their politics, and their own self-aggrandizement. Josiah Walls experienced these interest pressures during his three terms in the United States House of Representatives. His effort to accommodate these pressures and, at the same time, avoid complete dependence on any one, provides the backdrop to a discussion of his public career on a national level.

To understand what motivated Walls and his black peers to press for change on specific issues in the manner they did, one must first understand the prevailing black political ideology that had been formulated by the end of the war. The commonly held black view of political rights and human equality was based on the Declaration of Independence and the political traditions of the eighteenth century. In accordance with the time-honored philosophy of the universal rights of men, the black leaders of Reconstruction, including Walls, accepted the belief that the end of the "peculiar institution" restored to their race the natural and inalienable rights of all citizens. To John Mercer Langston such a belief affirmed the inherent sovereignty of the people and their political rights.[5] Protection of those rights required political power in government. Government without a voice in the selection of its officers constituted tyranny. This line of reasoning accounted for the continual push by black leaders for the franchise for the mass of black people.

Ignorance borne in generations of servitude has never been an instructor in the use of the franchise when gained; thus, the black congressmen, especially Walls, also made strong and urgent appeals for wide-

4. *From Slavery to Freedom: A History of the Negro Americans*, pp. 319–21.
5. *Freedom and Citizenship, Selected Lectures*, pp. 109–11, 119–20.

spread public education. Their racial ideology also pointed at the complete integration of Negroes into the American mainstream, and further illustrations were based on the superiority of American institutions and the wisdom found in the Christian ethic of the brotherhood of man. As a result, it was a common practice to show the rest of American society the contrasts between its ideals and the realities of the black position therein, as the *New Orleans Tribune*, a black newspaper, stressed when it noted that "all discrimination on account of birth or origin is repugnant to the principles of our government and to American manners and customs." Yet black people, the paper felt, remained "enveloped in a law of proscription."[6]

However, the black politicians were not urging what came to be defined in this period as social equality. Congressman James H. Rainey of South Carolina noted the difference between social and political equality for the benefit of his white listeners: "I venture to assert to my fellow white citizens that we, the colored people, are not in quest of social equality. . . . I do not ask to be received into your family circles if you are not disposed to receive me there."[7] P. B. S. Pinchback, the lieutenant governor of Louisiana, hastened to label any statement to the contrary a "wholesale falsehood."[8] The significance of this ideological framework lay in the blacks' fear that most white Americans were satisfied with conditions now that slavery no longer existed. Evidence in support of their assumption was clear. The American Anti-Slavery Society, for example, met in its final session only a few days after ratification of the Thirteenth Amendment. And if white abolitionists were committed to the Negro's cause during Reconstruction, they still were few in number.[9]

The black representatives to Congress in Reconstruction also understood they reflected more than a Negro electorate, even if most prejudiced whites believed otherwise. Indeed, Walls and his colleagues were forced to respond to a wider range of people and interests, pressures and issues, than those tied only to race. From 1869 to 1877, the period covered by the Forty-first to the Forty-fourth Congresses, black congressmen were elected from the following states: six from South Carolina, three from Alabama, and one each from Florida, Georgia, Louisiana,

6. July 8, 1865.

7. *Congressional Record*, 43d Cong., 2d sess., pp. 958–60.

8. John Hope Franklin, *Reconstruction after the Civil War*, p. 91.

9. James M. McPherson, *The Struggle for Equality: Abolitionists and the Negro in the Civil War and Reconstruction*, passim.

and North Carolina, and two United States senators from Mississippi. Although it has been accepted for a long time that black popular majorities achieved at the expense of white disfranchisement elected these men, white disfranchisement never approached the major proportions popularized in the early accounts of Reconstruction. In Florida, for example, the net effect of white disfranchisement was a loss of 156 votes. Moreover, the available census data show that Mississippi and South Carolina had a larger black than white population in 1860. Louisiana reached the same proportion by 1870, and Georgia, Florida, and Alabama had populations over 40 per cent black. However, only South Carolina and Florida managed to register more black voters than white under the provisions of the Military Reconstruction Act of 1867.[10] In Walls' case, the closeness of his election victories alone calls into question the assumption that his base of support was of only one color. Events proved that Negroes did not dominate the second electoral district in Florida. It seems clear that the black congressmen who committed themselves to nonracial issues did so in response to their diverse electorates.

There were four general categories of congressional activity that interested Josiah Walls: education, civil rights, foreign affairs (relating to the Cuban insurrection), and internal improvements. Outside these issues, little else is known about his work. He served on three minor committees while in the House, those of expenditures in the navy department, state militia organizations, and mileage for members of Congress. He introduced no legislation as a result of his committee work nor are the records of his participation in committee available. Therefore, one is reduced to an examination of his efforts on the floor of the House, an admittedly less than satisfactory measure of assessing his career as a congressman. According to some historians, Walls was ill equipped to handle the important issues of the day, but he did well enough under the limitations of his lack of education. An analysis of Walls' participation during the complicated and lengthy debate concerning the proposed establishment of a national education fund reveals that despite his educational disadvantage he clearly was capable of following and sifting through complex arguments.

On January 15, 1872, Legrand Perce of Mississippi, chairman of the House committee on education and labor, reported a bill from his committee to the Forty-second Congress calling for the establishment of

10. Forrest G. Wood, "On Revising Reconstruction History: Negro Suffrage, White Disfranchisement, and Common Sense."

a national education fund financed by the United States public lands.[11] The bill proposed a comprehensive program insuring that all children between the ages of six and sixteen would be guaranteed a free public school education. Among its more controversial sections, the bill established the office of a federal superintendent of education charged with the responsibility of enforcing the act; it provided that all revenue from the public lands was to be used to swell the fund; it stipulated that the division of monies from the fund would depend upon population; and finally, that the revenue from the fund could be used for no other purpose. Perce explained the general intent of the legislation: "I know it would be impracticable and unwise to supersede the present system of State instruction. The bill submitted does not attempt anything of the kind. On the other hand, it encourages and strengthens the State systems of education under the authority of the States and through their political organizations."[12]

There was immediate opposition to the bill, primarily Democratic and nonsectional. Some opponents of the measure felt legitimate concern that it far exceeded the constitutional authority of the federal government. Other representatives from both North and South were adamant against any sort of appropriation for the education of Negroes. John T. Bird of New Jersey expressed serious concern that the bill would surrender unusually and dangerously strong power to a single federal official, the commissioner of education. "It will be observed," Bird said, "that this provision places in the hands of a single officer . . . absolute and entire control of this fund. . . . Are we prepared to sanction any such legislation as this—any such concentration of power?"[13] The whole question of federal usurpation of the reserved powers of the states to control their own systems of education centered on this issue. The proponents of the fund could offer no constitutional support for the concept of a national education system beyond a sympathetic expression of the principle that general education and the nation's well-being were implicitly tied together by the Preamble of the Constitution. John B. Storm of Pennsylvania argued the bill misconstrued the primary purpose of the public lands, which was to provide "cheap homes and cheap farms for the poor man." He also touched upon the political nature of the bill, noting that "it has been hinted here that this bill will be of particular benefit to the southern States. We know what that means. It means

11. *Congressional Globe*, 42d Cong., 2d sess., p. 396.
12. Ibid., pp. 535, 564–66.
13. Ibid., pp. 791–92.

southern votes for the bill." To offset the southern leaning toward passage, Storm appealed to southern bias and raised the spectre of race-mixing in the schools. He called the bill a "Trojan horse. In its interior are [sic] concealed the lurking foe—mixed schools. Though I am no prophet, yet, I venture to say, in less than one year from now, if you pass this bill, you will see an amendment to it compelling the States to educate the races in the same schools."[14] Storm's inflammatory attack was amplified by Henry D. McHenry of Kentucky. He pursued the economic foolishness behind the racial "nightmare" of integrated education. McHenry figured school districts in each state would benefit by no more than $6 to $8 per child from the fund and that each state would receive no more than $100,000, a small enough sum for an ambitious project. "And, sir, we do not propose to educate the negro children between the ages of six and sixteen, in order to receive [that amount]. . . . We would have to tax ourselves to the extent of $1,000,000 annually to set up and carry on a system of common schools for the negroes. It would be an independent system from the one we now have for we do not intend to establish a system of mixed schools, leading to a social equality of the races."[15]

The prejudices of the opposition almost obscured the fact that the nation needed to do something about its education. There was little doubt the education systems of the southern states needed some kind of boost. Both Legrand Perce and George Hoar of Massachusetts suggested that the bill in large measure could improve upon the educational stimulus already being provided by the Peabody Fund, and the latter especially emphasized the illiteracy rate in the South. According to the 1870 census, Florida, for example, contained almost 72,000 illiterate people out of its total population of about 187,000. Of the former figure approximately 53,000 were black, while some 27,000 people of both races under twenty-one years of age were unable to read or write. Hoar indicated similar conditions prevailed in the other southern states.[16]

On February 3, 1872, Walls stood up to answer Georgia Congressman Archibald McIntyre's assault on the invasion of state rights occasioned by the bill. He leaned on the fallacious thought in the Conservative argument: "We know what the cry about State Rights means, and more especially when we hear it produced as an argument against the establishment of a fund for the education of the people. Judging from the past,

14. Ibid., pp. 564–66, 568–69.
15. Ibid., pp. 788–89.
16. Ibid., pp. 591–93.

I must confess that I am somewhat suspicious of such rights knowing, as I do, that the Democratic party in Georgia, as well as in all of the other southern States, have been opposed to the education of the negro and poor white children." In expressing his support for the bill, Walls marshaled the black ideology about government, citizen rights, and protection. "I am in favor, Mr. Speaker, of not only this bill, but of a national system of education, because I believe that the National Government is the guardian of the liberties of all its subjects. And having within a few years ago incorporated into the body-politic a class of uneducated people, the majority of whom, I am sorry to say are colored, the question for solution and the problems to be solved, then, are: can these people protect their liberties without education; and can they be educated under the present condition of society in the States where they were when freed? . . . Imagine, I say, your race today in this deplorable situation. Would you be considered as comprehending their desires and situation, were you to admit that their former enslavers would take an impartial interest in their educational affairs? I think not."[17] Although Walls had stressed the universal importance of education in his speech, there were two other significant points. First, he was determined to position the discussion of the bill on a racial plane. The speech reveals the intensity of his feeling that education was a major key to racial advancement. In conjuring the possible obverse in the conditions of the races in slavery, Walls was expressing a rather modern view that racial inferiority rested on inferior racial opportunities, not inferior racial characteristics. Second, the speech signaled those Republicans who desired to "wave the bloody shirt" in front of their Democratic opponents that the issue of commitment to education could be a viable target. In any event, Walls' reply to McIntyre marks one of his major moments on the floor of Congress.

Following Walls' speech, voting on the bill and a number of amendments began. An amendment was passed that specified that this bill would in no way interfere in the use of the public lands for homesteaders. Another important proviso passed correcting the distribution procedure of the funds. It was agreed the monies from the fund would be distributed for the first ten years on a basis of the percentage of illiterate people in a state, rather than on its total population. This insured the southern states would receive the major portion. If the money had been distributed by total population, the result would have been skewed heavily

17. Ibid., pp. 808–10.

toward the more populous, wealthier, more educated northeastern states.

Although all of these amendments improved the operation of the bill, it was the last amendment attached which guaranteed congressional approval. This provided that funds could not be withheld because a state established segregated school districts.[18] Walls voted for all save this last.

It also was clear to another black congressman that the debate over the national educational fund had assumed a particular tone because of the racial fears and prejudices involved. James Rainey reflected on the intensity of feeling which had been aroused against the bill: "It is truly marvelous to observe the manifest antipathy exhibited toward measures [that have] for their purpose the amelioration and improvement of the masses. . . . In my opinion, if the doctrine of State rights was not destroyed in the heated conflict of the late war, there are little or no apprehensions of such a contingency in the passage of this bill."[19] The final vote on the bill, with amendments, was 117 to 98, with 24 abstentions.[20]

In the course of their speeches on the education bill, Walls and Rainey touched upon the lack of commitment to racial advancement, but nowhere was this lack more evident than on the issue of civil rights. In December 1871, Walls introduced House Bill 734, which specified his intent to remove all disabilities on Floridians affected by the Fourteenth Amendment. He asked that his bill be attached as a rider to the supplementary civil rights bill sponsored by Charles Sumner.[21] Joe M. Richardson has suggested, as it has been suggested also for the other blacks in Congress during this period, that the emphasis by Negroes placed upon general amnesty for former Confederates manifested Walls' desire to "cement relations" between the races.[22] While it is likely this indeed was the primary motive for individual relief bills sponsored during each session, it is an unlikely explanation for general amnesty. Walls meant to join general amnesty and civil rights. Washington's *New National Era* called special attention to his bill's "coupling therein amnesty . . . with provisions securing to the outraged colored man the advantages and securities contained in Senator Sumner's bill supplementary to the Civil Rights Bill. We thank Mr. Walls for this happy suggestion. He deserves the thanks and support not only of his colored

18. Ibid., p. 882.
19. Ibid., appendix.
20. Ibid., pp. 902–3.
21. Ibid., p. 198.
22. *The Negro in the Reconstruction of Florida*, p. 188.

constituents in Florida, but of every colored man in the nation . . . [and] he deserves consideration at the hands of every lover of justice."[23] What Walls had done by initiating this particular strategy was to attempt the exchange of civil rights and amnesty on a quid pro quo basis so as to improve racial conditions. The strategy was founded on the recognition that white supremacy was stronger than black demands, and it was consistent also with the belief that integration was the ultimate goal. As the *New National Era* pointed out, Walls' bill tied generosity toward disfranchised whites to justice for blacks. Of equal significance, however, the bill reflected the black perspective of the view held by white politicians in the Republican party on the two issues.

But the issues of rights and amnesty were moving a different current of sentiment among white Republicans. It was true that President Grant had raised the subject of a general amnesty in his annual message to Congress at the outset of its second session in 1871. He had asked if it were "not now the time that the disabilities imposed by the fourteenth amendment should be removed."[24] Thus, Walls was implementing at least in part the wish of the administration. The *New National Era* suggested: "If our worthy President and the Republican party shall think it timely and best to grant amnesty to those that rebelled, let it be so, but justice calls on them to secure, at the same time, the respect and security in civil rights to the colored man."[25] Despite Grant's sentiment, it appeared the Republican party intended for the controversial twin issues to run a different political course.

The Democratic party had made substantial gains in its number of congressional seats as a result of the 1870 elections.[26] It had gained, for example, five seats in the House from Pennsylvania and three from New Hampshire, as well as seats from West Virginia, Wisconsin, New York, Indiana, Illinois, Nevada, and Michigan. As G. Selden Henry has suggested, Grant could easily have been influenced by the political returns; certainly the Democratic upsurge in Congress helps explain the thrust for amnesty at this time.[27]

During a Senate speech on January 26, 1872, Charles Sumner attached his supplementary civil rights bill to a general amnesty bill. He argued

23. December 23, 1871.
24. James D. Richardson, *A Compilation of the Messages and Papers of the Presidents, 1789–1902*, 7:153.
25. December 23, 1871.
26. George H. Mayer, *The Republican Party, 1854–1966*, p. 179.
27. "Radical Republican Policy toward the Negro during Reconstruction, 1862–1872," passim.

that "since the removal of disabilities is now passed, it is essential that justice to the colored fellow citizens should accompany this generosity."[28] Because any amendment to the Constitution required a two-thirds vote, the result of Sumner's action was to force the same proviso on the civil rights bill. Following a tie vote and the deciding ballot cast in its favor by the vice president, Schuyler Colfax, Sumner's proposal to attach the two measures succeeded.[29] Although Sumner, Walls, and a few other radical and black congressmen wished both provisions would pass, most Republicans did not. It was expedient to vote for Sumner's proposal, however, because Republicans, wanting to avoid an even larger Democratic vote (the inevitable result of amnesty) and uncommitted to civil rights, knew that the package would be unacceptable to two-thirds of Congress.

The *New York Tribune* analyzed the Republican motives in this fashion, remarking that "such men as Morton, Conkling, Edmunds, Nye, and Chandler . . . are suddenly converted to Sumner's way of thinking, because it is the only way amnesty can be defeated without appearing to oppose the President."[30] However, the pressure for amnesty was too great to be put off. When Benjamin Butler introduced another general amnesty bill in the House of Representatives on May 13, it passed by the necessary margin. This came after a second attempt to couple civil rights and general amnesty. However, Butler resisted Legrand Perce's effort to repeat Sumner's technique. He justified his position with the following statement: "It is because we think the civil rights bill should pass, and can pass, by a majority, that we do not believe it is right to push that bill by fastening it upon a bill which requires a two-thirds vote. It should stand by itself, and for one, I propose to labor diligently to see a civil rights bill is passed, and that can be done by a majority of the House." It is interesting to note that Rainey and Robert Elliott, the black congressmen, were not allowed to express their objections until after the amnesty bill had passed.[31] Despite Butler's faith, the civil rights bill did not go into effect for another two years, and when it did it was little more than a shadow of Sumner's original legislation. In practice, it was only a dead letter of Reconstruction.[32]

Walls did concern himself with other, nonracially oriented issues. In such matters, especially internal improvement legislation, the young

28. *Congressional Globe*, 42d Cong., 2d sess., p. 622.
29. Ibid., p. 919.
30. January 24, 1872.
31. *Congressional Globe*, 42d Cong., 2d sess., pp. 3382–83, 3385.
32. David Donald, *Charles Sumner and the Rights of Man*, pp. 531–33.

congressman was much more successful in advancing both the interests of Florida and his own ends. In all of his several sessions, Walls remained a consistent champion of internal improvements for his state. For example, in the third session of the Forty-second Congress alone, he introduced bills to establish customhouses, post offices, courthouses, and other federal buildings in Jacksonville, Cedar Key, and Key West.[33] In the Forty-third Congress, he added bills to improve the St. Johns River, the Apalachicola River, and the harbors at Key West and Pensacola, as well as a general bill for the improvement of other harbors and rivers in Florida.[34] Moreover, he introduced successful legislation that secured seven new mail routes for the state.[35] As a result of his efforts in this direction, Walls was lauded by several Florida newspapers and has been described as a "booster" of Florida and a "zealous advocate" of its interests.[36] However, it must be pointed out that he also advocated his own personal interests in at least two specific instances concerning internal improvement legislation.

In the last session of the Forty-third Congress, Walls introduced legislation that granted chunks of the public lands in Florida to a canal and steamship company that had been incorporated to construct a cross-state canal from Fernandina on the Atlantic to the Gulf of Mexico; thus, shipping could move on to New Orleans. The commercial advantages to Florida were obvious, and Walls himself pushed for the project in an appearance before the Senate transportation committee on January 28, 1874. In his appeal for the project, Walls called for the federal government to exercise "paternal care" in allotting resources from the public lands for internal improvements. His speech before the Windom committee was well received. The *Florida Union* reported it with the added comment "Mr. Walls adds his mite to what has gone before and does it well."[37] In fact, he won the outright admiration of the paper, especially in contrast to the other members of the Florida delegation. "In all the play so far, except for the effort of Mr. Walls . . . [the Florida congressional delegation] has been as dumb as lambs bound and corded for the slaughter pen."[38] However, Walls himself would have benefited directly

33. *Congressional Globe*, 42d Cong., 3d sess., index.
34. Ibid., 43d Cong., 1st sess., index.
35. Ibid., 42d Cong., 2d sess., p. 3939.
36. Richardson, *The Negro in the Reconstruction of Florida*, pp. 179–80.
37. (Jacksonville) *Florida Union*, February 5, 1874; U.S. Congress, *Report of the Select Committee on Transportation Routes to the Seaboard*, 43d Cong., 1st sess., pp. 954–55. The committee was chaired by Senator William Windom of Minnesota.
38. *Florida Union*, March 12, 1874.

from federal grants to the canal company, as he was one of the incorporators listed when the bill authorizing the company came before the
Florida legislature in 1873. There were other familiar names, both
friends and foes of Walls, including Robert Meacham, James H. Roper,
John R. Scott, and even "Little Giant" Dennis.[39] In this instance, Walls'
interest in his state merged completely with his own ends.

The same conflict, or coincidence, of interest applied to his offering a
bill for public lands to the Great Southern Railway Company in 1871;
indeed, it was the very first bill introduced by Walls as a freshman
congressman. It was designed to help finance a railroad to run the entire
length of the state, from the St. Marys River on the north to Key West,
and then to connect with other transportation to Cuba and other nearby
West Indian islands.[40] The Great Southern Railway Company was a
fraud, and it seems incredible that Walls would not have known it.
According to the available evidence, he was a member of the original
board of incorporators for the railroad company and was listed as receiv-
ing $150,000 worth of stock subscription in the company. The Florida
legislature had approved the act of incorporation on November 24, 1870,
following an affirmative vote for the plan by the trustees of the internal
improvement funds. According to the provisions of its approved charter,
the Great Southern Railway Company was to receive from the state's
internal improvement fund alternate 10-mile sections of land on either
side of the proposed route, and another 5-mile swath if the land were
improved.[41] The company was capitalized at $10 million, divided
among nineteen men, four of whom were also members of the board of
trustees of the internal improvement fund.

A bill for a federal subsidy to the company had been sponsored
originally by Sen. Thomas Osborn and Representative Charles Hamilton in the Forty-first Congress. However, either Hamilton was offered a
bribe to move the bill along in the House, or else he attempted to
blackmail the company for the same end. When the scandal broke in the
spring of 1871, both explanations were put forth. According to Hamilton, he had been approached by A. C. Osborn, a Brooklyn-based
clergyman and brother of the Florida senator. To push a bill through the
House, Osborn allegedly offered Hamilton $1 million in subscribed
stock, a position as permanent attorney for the company at an annual

39. *Fernandina Observer*, January 18, 1873.
40. *Congressional Globe*, 42d Cong., 1st sess., p. 79.
41. *Minutes of the Board of Trustees, Internal Improvement Fund of the State of Florida*,
pp. 443–47.

retainer of $5,000, and an appointment, to be secured by Senator Osborn, as United States marshal.[42] Hamilton denied the countercharge by Osborn that these were the conditions demanded in return for his support, and he refused to aid the bill at all.

There are two possible reasons behind the split between the Osborns and Hamilton. First, Hamilton was opposed to the Republican decision to dump him in favor of a black nominee for Congress in 1870. It should be remembered that the Osborn faction at the August 1870 meeting had stood behind Robert Meacham for the bid, while Hamilton remained a serious contender. Second, the conflict may have centered on Hamilton's wish to be appointed as a United States marshal in Florida. The position was held at the time by Thomas Wentworth, a longtime friend of Osborn. According to the *Washington Capital*, the problem involved in replacing Wentworth with Hamilton was "the immediate cause of the rupture" between the two congressmen.[43] Eventually, the United States Senate rejected Hamilton's nomination as postmaster at Jacksonville. Neither Walls in the House nor Osborn supported it.[44]

Walls reinitiated the Great Southern subsidy as his first official legislative action, and it seems quite likely that he became a stockholder in the company precisely for that purpose: he had been elected to replace Hamilton in Congress prior to the date of incorporation. In any event, the railway charter was revoked by the trustees of the internal improvement fund on January 16, 1872. The major complaint against the company was that "no work has yet been done in fulfillment of the conditions of the grant, nor any evidence of the purpose or ability of the company to do so." In its revocation, the board also stated that the grants to the company from the swamp and overflowed lands administered by the fund were in excess of the 6-mile sections specified in the state charter.[45]

When it came to other such railway grants, Walls, while in Congress, was far more careful. For example, on June 7, 1872, he objected strenuously to a bill giving the American Fork Railway the right-of-way through 17 miles of public land in the Utah Territory. According to his reading of the charter, Walls believed the federal government would

42. *Tallahassee Sentinel*, April 15, 1871. It should be noted that A. C. Osborn was the only man who happened to be a member of both the Florida and the Georgia Great Southern companies. It had been planned that the road would connect with the North through Georgia, but the Georgia company's route did not pass through public land. Therefore, no subsidy from Congress was necessary.

43. April 9, 1871.

44. *New York Tribune*, February 1, 1872.

45. *Minutes of the Board of Trustees, Internal Improvement Fund*, pp. 468–70.

have become obligated to guarantee the company's bonds at $20,000 per mile. William S. Holman of Indiana, a supporter of the bill, replied: "Nobody would ever dream that the Government could be made responsible for the debts of this corporation. This bill is of a class, of which we have passed several during the past weeks, conferring upon corporations organized under territorial legislation this power to mortgage their roads."[46] Walls won the debate; the bill went back to committee.

On December 8, 1873, the issue of civil rights came again to the fore. In another attempt to delay congressional action on the measure, Representative Williard of Vermont recommended the bill be referred to the judiciary committee for further study. Williard argued that he personally was unprepared to vote for a bill "which I have had no opportunity of reading." Walls was angered by Williard's remark, and he replied to the Vermont congressman in the strongest terms: "It is a bill which has been before Congress, and this House, for the last two years, and every member of this House . . . is well acquainted with it; and I hope it will not be refused. We did not ask that the amnesty bill should be referred to a committee, and all we ask is that the same justice shall be done to us." Walls also objected to allowing Alexander Stephens, the former Confederate vice president and now a congressman from Georgia, to take part in an hour-long civil rights debate with Robert Elliott of South Carolina. Walls felt it was an issue upon which others might have wished to express opinions, and the time for each speaker should have been limited. However, on the advice of "friends," he withdrew his objection.[47]

Walls somewhat diverged from state or racial leanings to pronounce his position regarding the Cuban insurrection in the Ten Years War. Like many prominent white supporters in favor of recognizing belligerent status for the rebels under de Cespedes, Walls couched his support in moral terms.[48] His view of the situation is important because it is the only major speech on the issue by a black congressman in this period. Walls introduced a joint resolution in support of Cuban belligerency in December 1873, and made a lengthy speech in its behalf the following January. In a moving and dramatic effort, he adduced the major events and the great revolts of history to support the Cuban patriotic right to revolt against Spanish oppression: "The progress of the human

46. *Congressional Globe*, 42d Cong., 2d sess., p. 4331.

47. Ibid., 43d Cong., 1st sess., p. 97.

48. Allan Nevins, *Hamilton Fish: The Inner History of the Grant Administration*, and Lester D. Langley, *The Cuban Policy of the United States: A Brief History*, provide full treatments of the entire Cuban affair.

family is indicated all along the line of its march by bright epochs, embodied in the heroic endeavor of peoples in the upbuilding of self-government, and in opposition to the pernicious habit of government under the extinct prerogative of divine right." He illustrated his meaning by reference to "the continental patriots of our own land [who] arose in their honesty, their might and majesty, and their devotion to truth and justice, to throw off the yoke of a tyranny. . . . Then came the struggle of the peoples of the Spanish possessions in South and Central America to throw off the [same] yoke. . . . The Greek rebellion is another instance of the revolt of the people against oppression." Walls suggested the brutality, injustice, and oppression in these examples paled beside the conditions under Spanish rule in Cuba. Moreover, he carefully pointed out that while "contributions of money, the necessaries of life, and the munitions of war" went to the Greek rebels, and the fledgling Spanish states in South America were protected by the Monroe Doctrine, "the conditions of neutrality still the best impulses of the heart and paralyze the strong that was ever ready to protect the weak and assist the oppressed to a higher plane of manhood." He castigated Spain for its continued slavery in Cuba despite the emancipation act of June 23, 1870. He dismissed that act as "an excellent sample of the buncombe and subterfuge which attempt to foist upon the world a bastard republic, which, under the plea of Spanish pride, tolerates the most horrible crimes against humanity, and protects with all the power of the government an institution repugnant to every sense of decency and right."

Walls also took note of the Spanish argument that recognition of belligerent status was contrary to international law because there was no war, only a civil insurrection. The American secretary of state, Hamilton Fish, had endorsed and expanded this argument by pointing out to President Grant that the rebels, although espousing a popular cause, were not as yet successful enough in the prosecution of the resistance to warrant belligerent status from the United States.[49] According to Walls, since "the Spanish government has continued to suppress the Cuban rebellion . . . every year since its inception, at the cost of twenty thousand lives and hundreds of thousands in treasure . . . [then] in God's name let us interpose to save Spain and the so-called Spanish republic." Walls closed his speech by presenting to the House a resolution in support of the recognition of belligerent status for the Cuban rebels, passed by the Florida legislature, which urged the United States government to "extend such aid to the people of Cuba as becomes a great

49. Nevins, *Hamilton Fish*, p. 181.

republic, whose people so ardently sympathize with an oppressed nation."[50]

Perhaps as nowhere else in the country, there was an internal political implication in the strong support given by the Florida delegation in Congress. J. W. Locke, United States district judge at Key West, stated the crux of the political ramifications in a letter to Senator Osborn: "I am somewhat fearful of the result of the ensuing election in [Key West] unless we manage to influence or control the vote of the Cubans here who are, under our laws, permitted to vote. They have some 400 votes and hold the balance of power."[51] In turn, Osborn was even more outspoken in suggesting to New Hampshire Sen. William E. Chandler, member of the national Republican executive committee, that he would "willingly advocate their interest in the next session."[52] The conservative Tallahassee *Weekly Floridian* mused over Congressman William Purman's purpose in warmly espousing the Cuban cause: "Were we disposed to be uncharitable, we might suspect Purman of designs on the Cuban vote at Key West as the animating cause of his labors on behalf of Cuban independence."[53]

In defense of Walls and his fellow Florida congressmen, it should be noted that Florida's proximity to Cuba and its own Spanish heritage, as well as the Cuban voters in Key West, account for the local interest in the situation. Furthermore, the well-organized propaganda campaign carried on by the Cuban junta stimulated support.[54] As a black man and an ex-slave himself, Walls certainly was in sympathy with anyone who resisted oppression. Finally, Grant himself was inclined toward awarding belligerent status to the Cubans, and many Republicans felt they were in harmony with the administration on this issue.

There was one issue about which Walls expressed an opinion untouched by either racial, partisan, or personal concerns. This was in his speech in favor of a congressional appropriation for the 1876 centennial celebration. In defense of a proposed $3 million grant for the exposition at Philadelphia, Walls touched the quintessence of the black dream, the healing of sectional bitterness and the molding of the nation's unity. He envisioned the centennial celebration as the gathering place for "the immensity of the mineral resources of this favored country, of which the simple and truthful report has amazed the world—our incalculable

50. *Congressional Globe*, 43d Cong., 1st sess., appendix.
51. J. W. Locke to Thomas Osborn, October 14, 1872, Chandler Papers, vol. 32.
52. Osborn to William Chandler, December 2, 1872, ibid.
53. June 30, 1874.
54. Nevins, *Hamilton Fish*, pp. 179–80.

wealth of coal, iron, copper, silver, and gold. . . . The admitted perfection in the cultivation of various of the mechanic arts, the demonstrated excellence of mechanical skill attained by our American workmen . . . the wide-spread and familiar use of steam and other machinery in the prosecution of all varieties of agricultural as well as merely mechanical work . . . a full exhibition of the immense variety of the natural productions of the United States, stretching as it does from the tepid waters of the Gulf to the northern home of the glaciers, and reaching from the orange and grape of California, the banana, the cocoa-nut, and the pine-apple of Florida, to the dwarfed and stinted vegetation of the Polar circle . . . will present at one glance so striking and palatable a view of the immense extent of our country . . . in what will ultimately and organically, in no distant period, form a solid continuation of coterminous States, as to sustain universal and irresistable attention."

Walls closed his last major speech on a philosophic note: "Long ago patriotism was said by an eminent English novelist to be 'the love of office,' and politics 'the art of getting it'; and I am not ignorant of the common supposition that, in southern politics particularly, the actual truth . . . [of the] allegation is being continually illustrated; but the centennial is not the least attractive or the least important feature of it, in the estimation of southern men, 'without respect to previous condition.' . . . In the face of the common drift of the modern general mind toward ridicule of anything in the way of sentiment in the discussion of important questions, I am fully conscious that I am . . . ascribing to a patriotic attachment to one's own country, its people, and its government." Walls' closing statement clearly expressed the nineteenth-century blacks' view of their ultimate role and goal in American society: "So I believe that when from every corner of this broad land, from every State and Territory, thousands and millions of free citizens of a free government shall assemble in the very cradle and place of birth of all . . . they hold dear, and exchange with each other the mutual grasp and the meaningful glances of common citizenship, there will be aroused in the bosoms of all a higher and purer sense of the honest and sincere attachment cherished by all in common for those free institutions . . . and which will strengthen all the bonds which can unite freemen to their native land, and will kindle a blaze . . . in whose dazzling light all questions of differences and all hurtful recollections . . . will be blotted out."[55]

55. *Congressional Globe*, 43d Cong., 1st sess., appendix.

6

Inside the National
Negro Convention

THE fact that Josiah Walls often acted apart from the Republican party in his political career is, in part at least, a result of his having been a participant in the National Negro Convention movement during Reconstruction. It was within this all-black movement that many Negro politicians, including Walls, revealed the full depth of their disenchantment with Republican race policies. But their kind of critical awareness of the events of the post–Civil War period was only the continuation of a long tradition of Negro protest. The roots of the National Negro Convention lay in the seedbed of antebellum agitation over slavery and resistance to colonization. Founded originally in 1830 in response to the growing threat of the American Colonization Society, the Negro movement was eclipsed by the American Anti-Slavery Society in 1833, and it did not resurface until another decade had passed. During that hiatus, black leaders resolved to enlist and depend upon the support of white abolitionists to awaken "the sympathies and benevolence of the Christian, moral, and political world."[1] Among Negro organizations, the American Moral Reform Society replaced the National Negro Convention after 1835, advocating "moral suasion" as the rhetoric of progress. The new society turned toward moral and spiritual programs for Negro advancement. Nevertheless, it became apparent by the 1840s that racial advance and integration were impossible in an American society infected with slavery, sectional hostility, and prejudice. Nor had the white

1. National Negro Convention, 1835, *Minutes of the Fifth Annual Convention for the Improvement of the Free People of Colour in the United States*, p. 27.

abolitionist societies succeeded in altering the Negroes' status. In 1843 the National Negro Convention reconvened in Buffalo; four years later in Troy, New York, the movement dedicated itself to political agitation and criticism.[2]

At the same time, it also experienced a brief flirtation with voluntary emigration. Although the American Colonization Society had been its chief opponent for years, a new attitude toward emigration had appeared among many blacks. There were several reasons for the awakening interest. With the Liberian Declaration of Independence in 1847, a black nation supplanted the white American Colonization Society as an authority on African life. The enactment of the Fugitive Slave Law in 1850 destroyed the hopes and optimism of the black leadership. Coupled with this was their disappointment with the efforts of the white antislavery societies. Negroes were excluded from membership in some of them and exercised only symbolic roles in others.[3] As a result of these conditions, emigrationist thinking became more popular. At the 1854 meeting of the National Negro Convention in Cleveland, a young black physician, Martin R. Delany, dominated the delegates' attention. Delany, who had traveled extensively in West Africa, had developed a strong attachment to emigration. In the convention he argued that neither citizenship nor freedom were applicable concepts for Negro Americans: "Our oppressors are ever gratified at our manifest satisfaction, especially when that satisfaction is founded on false premises; an assumption on our part of the enjoyment of rights and privileges which have never been conceded, and which, according to the present system of United States policy, we can never enjoy." According to Delany, emigration was the opportunity to shake off the burden of white supremacy by "grasping hold of those places where chance is in their [the Negroes'] favor, and establishing the rights and power of the colored race."[4]

Yet, this type of thinking ended abruptly with the onset of war. Throughout the early period of war the National Negro Convention lay

2. National Negro Convention, 1843, *Minutes of the National Convention of Colored Citizens: Held . . . for the Purpose of Considering Their Moral and Political Condition as American Citizens*. See also the following works of Howard H. Bell for a full understanding of the antebellum convention movement: "National Negro Conventions of the Middle 1840s: Moral Suasion vs. Political Action"; "The Negro Emigration Movement, 1849–1854: A Phase of Negro Nationalism"; "Expressions of Negro Militancy in the North, 1840–1860"; "A Survey of the Negro Convention Movement, 1830–1861."

3. John H. Bracey, Jr., August Meier, and Elliott Rudwick, eds., *Blacks in the Abolitionist Movement*, pp. 54–133.

4. Martin R. Delany, "Political Destiny of the Colored Race," in Frank A. Rollin, *Life and Public Services of Martin R. Delany*, pp. 327, 337.

dormant, but as a result of marked changes in the status of race, it was reactivated in 1864. Abolition of slavery had become a war aim. Black recruitment and combat illustrated the Negro's worth as an effective soldier. These two developments created an emotional mixture of enthusiasm and apprehension, for despite these changes, race prejudice and conservative race policies remained untouched. Colonization continued to be considered the only panacea. Even Lincoln found it attractive, fostering several proposals of his own design.[5] Meanwhile, at the same time that Frederick Douglass was saying the "Negro problem" would continue to be the nation's most severe until it "united upon some wise policy concerning it," eight blacks were convicted of illegally entering Illinois. Seven were sold or indentured to pay their fines.[6]

By 1864 some impact of change was felt. Black soldiers no longer were a composite spectre of horror, but stimulated excitement in some, acceptance in many. A *New York Times* reporter wrote: "There has been no more striking manifestation of the marvelous times that are upon us than the scene in our colored regiments. Had any man predicted it last year, he would have been thought a fool, even by the wisest and most discerning. History abounds with strange contrasts. It has always been an ever-shifting melodrama. But never, in this land at least, has it presented a transition so extreme."[7] This new spirit was felt in the National Negro Convention which reassembled in Syracuse in the fall of that year. Among the 144 black men who responded to the call in October was Jonathan Gibbs, future secretary of state in Florida, but at that time a Pennsylvania theologian. All the delegates agreed that "the present time is immeasurably more favorable than any other period in our history to unite and act for our own most vital interests."[8] Those who met in Syracuse were interested in achieving an effective racial program for the new Reconstruction, and to carry it out they created the National Equal Rights League. Under the direction of John Mercer Langston, the Ohio abolitionist and lawyer who was to be elected to Congress from Virginia two decades later, the league was conceived as the practical arm of the National Negro Convention, carrying forth its programs and ideals. It reflected the basic need for unity and concerted action ex-

5. Lincoln's various colonization plans, which did not advocate compulsory deportation, were not favored by many Negroes. See Herbert Aptheker, ed., *A Documentary History of the Negro People in the United States*, pp. 471–75.

6. Joanne Grant, ed., *Black Protest: History, Documents, and Analyses, 1619 to the Present*, pp. 122–25.

7. March 7, 1864.

8. Aptheker, *A Documentary History*, p. 511.

pressed by most of the Syracuse delegates; its constitution pointed out that the Negro race could advance only through "a union of all energies and the use of all means in a given direction."[9]

Despite the hopes for the future and the spirit of the times, there was another sentiment heard in Syracuse that October. Some Negro leaders were disturbed by the political scene they surveyed. No vindication of black people was apparent. The politics of the Republicans and Democrats alike were suspect. Although a vast difference in the character and composition of the former was self-evident, the delegates had reservations about the party's commitment to racial progress. The convention published an address to the nation that compared the negative and reactionary attitude of the Republican party and the more active conservatism of the Democrats: ". . . it cannot be disguised, that while [the Democratic party] is our bitterest enemy, and is positively and actively reactionary, the Republican party is negatively and passively so in its tendency." The memorial condemned the Republican party for "its prevailing contempt for the character and rights of the colored race," and in doing so, it pointed specifically to its racial policies. The delegates were aware that the southern freedmen were devoid of rights or power, but they were unable to envision any change through "the plans emanating from this party for reconstructing the institutions of the Southern States." Their criticism extended even to abolition: "Even in the matter of the abolition of slavery . . . there is still room for painful doubt and apprehension. It is very evident that the Republican party, though a party composed of the best men of the country, is not prepared to make the abolition of slavery, in all the Rebel States, a consideration precedent to the reestablishment of the Union." Although Lincoln's Emancipation Proclamation had been in effect for almost two years, the Syracuse convention was unsure of its permanency. It was believed that a Republican Congress might reinstitute slavery, despite any potential objection from President Abraham Lincoln.[10]

The next gathering of the National Negro Convention was in Washington in January 1866, and the criticism and agitation for civil rights continued. In the midst of much political ferment, politics was again the chief concern of the delegates. During the two-year period since Syracuse, one goal had been realized. The war had ended, and the Thirteenth Amendment, effective December 18, 1865, had administered the final

9. Ibid., p. 526.
10. National Negro Convention, 1864, *Proceedings of the National Convention of Colored Men Held . . . October 4–7, 1864.*

blow to slavery. The more fragile executive order of Lincoln gave way to a lasting disposition of the "peculiar institution."

Congress at this time, however, had before its members three important proposals—the renewal of the Freedmen's Bureau Bill, a civil rights measure, and pending legislation that became the Fourteenth Amendment. Despite the critical importance of these issues, most of the interest in the convention centered upon the new president, Andrew Johnson. He was an unknown quantity to the delegates. Lincoln was a Republican; Johnson was not. Whereas Lincoln came from the Midwest, Johnson had been a poor white from the South. Although aware of his staunch unionist sentiments, the convention wished to ascertain the new president's views on the "negro question."

Several delegates, including Joseph Oates, the controversial "congressman" from Tallahassee, met with the president at the White House on February 7, 1866. After the usual round of civilities, Johnson began by expressing his friendship for Negroes. "If I know myself, and the feelings of my own heart," he explained, "they have been for the colored man." Yet, he could not hide his hostility. According to Johnson, he did not enjoy being "arraigned by some who can get up handsomely-rounded periods and deal in rhetoric, and talk about abstract ideas of liberty." His sympathies lay with the small, southern, non-slave-owning farmer. While the slave had at least gained his freedom, the small white farmer had nothing to show for having endured the conflict. Frederick Douglass, also present, touched upon the essence of the interview's significance at its conclusion. He realized the final answer to the "negro problem" lay within the race. The president had shown that there was no one else to depend upon.[11]

One prominent black not present at the interview, Martin R. Delany, working in the Freedmen's Bureau in Hilton Head, South Carolina, attached little hostility to Johnson's performance. After reading a newspaper account of the proceedings, Delany offered this advice to the assembled delegates in the convention: "Do not misjudge the President, but believe as I do, that he means to do right; that his intentions are good; that he is interested, among others of his fellow-citizens, in the welfare of the black man. . . . Do not expect too much of him—as black men, I mean. Do not forget that you are black and he is white. Make large

11. (Washington)*Daily National Intelligencer*, February 8, 1866. The fact that Joe Oates did actually appear at the White House conference is contrary to the traditional opinion that Oates never went more than a few miles from Florida before squandering his people's money and returning to Tallahassee, according to Davis, *Civil War and Reconstruction in Florida*, p. 428.

allowances for this, and take this as the standpoint."[12] But Johnson's private remarks following the session in the White House revealed the president's inner feelings. "Those damned sons of bitches," he exploded after the black delegates had left, "thought they had me in a trap! I know that damned Douglass; he's just like any nigger, and he would sooner cut a white man's throat than not."[13]

Many Republicans in 1866 wished to relegate the "negro question" to a secondary consideration. The governor of Maine, Samuel Cony, for example, reflected the opinion of many when he affirmed that while he supported Negro suffrage, he felt the timing to be improper: "I don't believe in making [it] an issue now. Our great object now is to secure the next Congress. If we don't get that, then all is lost; if we do get it, then all is safe. Therefore I am opposed to any changing of the issue."[14] It was a difficult situation. The black leaders in the convention movement realized their race was lost in the tangled political struggles of the "critical year." The scene was forbidding. Frederick Douglass castigated radicalism and the Republican party for their slowness, lack of commitment, and race policies. Surveying the scene in 1866, he wrote in the *Atlantic Monthly* that the Republican Congress, although "hotly charged" with radicalism, had renounced its power to secure rights to the Negroes, "with the obvious purpose to allow the rebellious States to disfranchise, if they should see fit, their colored citizens."[15]

On January 12, 1869, the National Negro Convention met again in the nation's capital, one day after a joint resolution proposing a constitutional amendment for impartial male suffrage had reached the floor of the House of Representatives. Because the delegates to the convention were sensitive to the effect of their presence upon the issue of suffrage, there was little strident criticism. A group of delegates did meet with President Grant. This committee reported his limited guarantee that "the colored people of the Nation may receive every protection which the law gives to them."[16]

Following this meeting, the National Negro Convention shifted its attention to other problems. After the passage of the Fifteenth Amend-

12. Rollin, *Life and Public Services of Martin R. Delany*, p. 281.
13. LaWanda Cox and John H. Cox, *Politics, Principles and Prejudice, 1865–1866: Dilemma of Reconstruction*, p. 163.
14. Howard K. Beale, *The Critical Year: A Study of Andrew Johnson and Reconstruction*, p. 178.
15. "Reconstruction," p. 761.
16. National Negro Convention, 1869, *Proceedings of the National Convention of the Colored Men of America*.

ment, agitation turned away from political reforms to press for economic relief. Although out of slavery, the Negro had become chained in new ways. In the South, the freedmen worked under harsh labor contracts which favored plantation owners and were enforced strictly by the Freedmen's Bureau. Moreover, the terrorist organizations and violent times tended to insure that black rights went unpracticed. In the North, the black worker also faced a new challenge: white labor had begun to organize. The growing number of unions were for "whites only"; the black workers were, for the most part, excluded.[17]

The whole issue of black and white working relationships during this period became critical. Although skilled labor comprised the main element of the labor movement, thereby effectively shutting out many black workers, enough Negroes worked in competitive trades to constitute a serious threat. Not all black people were poor and unskilled in this period. A special occupational census in 1865, for example, listed 100,000 black mechanics throughout the South while their white counterparts totaled one-fifth of that number. The categories included blacksmiths, gunsmiths, cabinetmakers, river pilots, and shipbuilders. In the North, there were also skilled and semiskilled Negroes.[18] These men, who were unable to join a union but needed to, stimulated demands for a Negro labor union. A March 1869 investigation by the *New York Times* into that city's working conditions uncovered "the most startling evidence of the powerful effect of prejudice." There Negroes were denied equal treatment, especially by the Irish element, a fact that had been "quietly acquiesced in by a very large portion of native-born citizens."[19] At the same time Lewis H. Douglass, son of the prominent black leader, was denied membership in the Columbia Typographical Union while employed in the Government Printing Office.[20] Several of the new unions excluded Negroes by written proviso in their constitutions, and the January 1869 call for a National Labor Union assembly in Washington invited delegates to attend from "every white trade or labor society."[21]

A few attempts to organize black workers were made. The *Washington Daily Morning Chronicle* reported: "Already the colored men, learning wisdom from their treatment by white trades union organizations, are

17. Sumner Eliot Matison, "The Labor Movement and the Negro during Reconstruction," pp. 426–68.
18. Charles H. Wesley, *Negro Labor in the United States*, p. 48.
19. March 2, 1869.
20. Wesley, *Negro Labor in the United States*, p. 168.
21. *Washington Daily Morning Chronicle*, December 18, 1869.

beginning to form similar associations of their own. . . . This is precisely what every sensible man has foreseen from the beginning of the proscription of colored men by the white organizations."[22] Finally, a call for a national convention on black labor's problems came from the Baltimore state labor meeting of Negroes held in July 1869. Under the driving influence of Isaac Myers, a Baltimore caulker and ardent champion of Negro unions, the National Negro Labor Convention met in Washington during the first week in December.

It was a large meeting. There were 203 accredited delegates from the District of Columbia and twenty-three states. Walls did not attend, but Florida's Negro workers were represented by Henry Harmon, John Scott of Jacksonville, Tallahassee carpenter Noah Graham, E. S. Francis, a carpenter from Palatka, and Thomas Harrold, a stevedore from Pensacola. Congressman Charles Hamilton and William J. Purman, then still with the Freedmen's Bureau, were among the visitors and guests. William U. Saunders, another of Walls' associates, somehow managed to attend the convention as the sole delegate from Nevada; indeed, he was the only delegate from west of the Mississippi. The committee on permanent organization reported a slate of officers, and Henry Harmon was elected assistant secretary. E. S. Francis was nominated for one of the vice presidencies. As the only "western" delegate, Saunders was also elected a vice president.[23] Temporary chairman was George T. Downing of Rhode Island, who, even in 1869, had begun opposing unqualified black support of the Republican party. In his address, he highlighted the critical weakness in the party: "The Republican party has been made an effective agent under God in liberating us from . . . chattel thralldom. We owe that party respect and support, in view of its agency in freeing us from that degradation." He added, however, that "it should have been more consistent, more positive in its dealings with our and our country's enemies. . . . When the ratification of the proposed fifteenth amendment to the Constitution shall have been effected, with what has already been accomplished in the same direction, much of the adhesive element which has made the composite Republican party a unit will have disappeared; for to hold together it must have attractive elements."[24]

Problems of the southern freedmen were also discussed. A plan was

22. Ibid., July 21, 1869.
23. National Negro Convention, 1869, *Proceedings of the Colored National Labor Convention*.
24. Ibid., p. 3.

put forth whereby free land in the public domain of the South could be awarded to Negroes. The records of the general land office, according to the convention's memorial to Congress, showed there to be 46,344,059 acres of public land in Alabama, Arkansas, Florida, Louisiana, and Mississippi. The memorial estimated that one-fourth (approximately 200,000) of the southern, able-bodied, male freedmen would avail themselves of the right of settlement. Each man might thus be given 40 acres of land, and still 38 million acres of public land would remain in the South.[25] During the convention's discussion of the problems in the South, Charles Hamilton offered the following resolution:

> Whereas, there exists in the Southern States—as one of the consequences of the institution of slavery—an organized "LAND MONOPOLY" which is baleful alike to domestic and national prosperity; and whereas extensive combinations have been entered into by the land owners in the South, for the purpose of maintaining said land monopoly, pledging themselves not to sell a foot of land, an implement of agriculture, or a farm animal to the freed people, with the willful, malicious design of keeping the freedmen in as dependent a position as possible, individually, socially, and politically; and whereas so long as this land monopoly prevails, the avenues of prosperity and personal independence are closed against the national freedmen; therefore be it
>
> Resolved, By the National Colored Labor Convention, That every possible legitimate measure be taken, in conjunction with the laboring masses of the country, to overthrow this cruel barrier to our progress—the monstrous "land monopoly" of the South.[26]

He went on to state that without some definite action against those southern conservatives who had managed to deflect any racial advancement beyond the single act of emancipation, "the prejudice, poverty, and the danger" would continue. It is possible that Hamilton's diatribe was meant to pander to the emotionalism of the moment on the convention floor. However, it is equally possible that the congressman meant exactly what he said; after all, he and Purman, both officers in the Marianna Freedmen's Bureau, had been physically assaulted by conservatives only a few months before.[27]

25. Ibid., p. 5.
26. Ibid., p. 32.
27. Ralph L. Peek, "Lawlessness and the Restoration of Order in Florida, 1868–1871," p. 117.

The convention took positive steps to deal with the economic conditions of black laborers. The National Negro Labor Union was established, accompanied by a Bureau of Labor designed to filter the national aims and programs down to local levels. State labor conventions were proposed. Walls' signature appeared over a call for a Florida labor convention to be held in Jacksonville on July 4, 1870. However, for some unknown reason, the meeting was postponed for two weeks. When it finally met, it was for the purpose of "forming a state organization and other objects of vital interest to the working men." Four delegates from each county were selected. Nothing else is known about this statewide attempt at unionism or Josiah Walls' efforts to bring it about.[28]

There was little more success on the national level. Financial destitution and political intrigue spelled ruin for the abortive attempt. At a second meeting of the National Negro Labor Union scheduled for January 9, 1871, Isaac Myers, president of the union, reported that while each of his state unions was in "flourishing condition," they could not afford to send delegates to the national convention. The national union folded shortly thereafter. Frederick Douglass took control in 1871, signaling the end to this period of Negro economic protest.[29]

By 1871, the leadership of the National Negro Convention had become convinced that the ballot was valueless without federal protection of the Negro's right to use it. Douglass expressed the feelings of many Negroes in demanding that Congress insure "a schoolhouse is placed at every cross-road of the South, and a bayonet between every ballot-box."[30] Yet white Republicans were busy with their own problems in 1871. As George Downing had suggested, the party was finding it difficult to maintain organizational integrity. Not able to assemble the necessary "attractive elements" Downing prescribed, Republican unity was breaking apart, and a serious rift had developed. The Liberal Republican movement, comprising those who opposed Grant's administrative excesses and a second presidential term, combined with Democrats to work against his reelection. This same factionalism was manifested in the National Negro Convention.

Whether pro- or anti-Grant, black leaders in 1871 were united in the belief that unqualified support and allegiance to the Republican party

28. *Tallahassee Sentinel*, June 11, 25, 1870. See Jerrell H. Shofner, "The Labor League of Jacksonville: A Negro Union and White Strikebreakers," for one example of black local efforts at union activity.
29. *Washington Daily Morning Chronicle*, January 14, 1871; Wesley, *Negro Labor in the United States*, pp. 187–88.
30. (Washington) *New National Era*, January 12, 1871.

were passé. Nearly all had at least some reservations about the party and its policies. Walls, for instance, had fashioned the "New Departure" group in Alachua County to express his disaffection with the regulars. But for most Negroes in this period, the political alternatives were limited. George Downing was one of the few blacks who felt that Democrats were entitled "to share with the Republican party the colored vote in the next Presidential election."[31]

Nevertheless, Downing's views were not popular. For most, the Republican party was the only viable choice. Frederick Douglass explained the intricacies of the problems in political alternatives for Negroes in 1871. It was his opinion that the Republicans had "overlooked and disregarded the claims" of Negroes and had assumed the black man "should be satisfied to vote for white men," an attitude brought about by their "well-known prejudice." However, the Democratic party offered no solace; of its race programs, Douglass remarked: "We are as a class murdered" by them. Independent politics would also result in failure. According to him, there was no party in view that would offer more to the Negro than the Republicans.[32]

Others also saw the tragedy in the Negroes' political position at that time. From his Freedmen's Bureau post at Hilton Head, Martin Delany delivered a scathing attack on Republican carpetbaggers in the South. He accused them of dividing the southern freedmen, and building political and personal fortunes "on deception, lying, cheating, and stealing." It was his opinion that the carpetbaggers were "the lowest grade of northern society, Negro haters at home." The black lieutenant governor of Louisiana, P. B. S. Pinchback, felt trapped "between the hawk of Republican demagogism and the buzzards of Democratic prejudice. The aspirants for position in our party threaten us with excommunication if we do not follow every jack o'lantern who raises his feeble light, and the Democrats invite us to annihilation if we turn away from these Republican jack o'lanterns." Pinchback's conclusion—"Truly ours is a great risk"—seemed to be the essence of the Negroes' problems.[33]

In the midst of this political ferment in 1871, a southern Negro convention met in Columbia, South Carolina. The atmosphere and conditions there could hardly have been less conducive for such a gathering. The delegates convened in the state legislature hall on October 18, one day after President Grant had declared martial law in the state in an

31. Ibid., June 8, 1871.
32. Philip S. Foner, *The Life and Writings of Frederick Douglass*, p. 75.
33. Elsie M. Lewis, "The Political Mind of the Negro, 1865–1900," p. 197.

attempt to suppress the Ku Klux Klan. Ostensibly, the convention was called to consider only local issues and problems. However, the events of the summer, especially the establishment of the liberal wing of the Republican party, forced the attention of the delegates to national concerns. Most of the delegates were disgruntled. During May, George Downing's disaffection became fullblown. He had written to the *New York Herald*, denouncing both regulars and liberals: "The mortification I feel in connection with the fact [the splinter group] is increased because those indifferent to the feelings of colored men . . . calculate on [their] vote."[34] On the other hand, Frederick Douglass took an entirely opposite position. In an editorial in the *New National Era*, he set himself squarely in the regular ranks of the party. "To desert [Grant] now, to refuse to sustain him, to seek in any way to weaken his influence, is the surest way to undo the work of the last ten years, and remand the Negro to a condition in some respects worse than that from which the Union delivered him. If we stand by President Grant and his administration, it is from no spirit of hero worship or blind attachment to mere party, but because in this hour there is no middle ground."[35]

Walls, Harmon, Gibbs, and Pearce were Florida's delegation to the Southern States Convention. However, Gibbs and Pearce were unable to attend. Even before the meeting got underway, some conservatives in the South already had impugned its motives. The editor of the *Macon Union*, although ostensibly Republican, accused the delegates of "plotting against whites" in their meeting. Douglass retorted that the Columbia gathering was not designed to attack whites. Rather, it was meeting "for the purpose of devising means for promoting the best interest of the race lately released from a condition almost dehumanizing."[36] This controversy exacerbated the feelings of many Negroes who perceived the paradox of an integrationist ideology in an all-black or "caste" convention. The lieutenant governor of South Carolina and permanent chairman of the convention, Alonzo J. Ransier, had been very reluctant to endorse the meeting because it "pointed to the assembling of a particular race—a component part of the American people." He wondered aloud "whether the colored men and the Republican party of the country could afford such a course."[37]

34. May 25, 1871.
35. April 6, 1871.
36. (Washington) *New National Era*, July 15, 1871.
37. Southern States Convention, 1871, *Proceedings of the Southern States Convention of Colored Men . . . 1871*, p. 9.

Walls, temporary chairman of the convention, was succeeded by Ransier. In his opening address, Ransier urged that only national issues should be considered, thereby avoiding sectional concerns and caste problems. The delegates, however, needed little such prompting. A spirited debate burst forth on an early resolution sponsored by Henry McNeal Turner of Georgia in support of the renomination of President Grant.[38] What followed over the next few days on the convention floor was the culmination of the growing black disaffection with the Republican party since 1864; this was evidenced as the delegates tried to hammer out an acceptable consensus concerning their role in the splintered party.

In reply to Turner's resolution, fellow Georgian John T. Quarles initiated the first attack on the regular Republicans. He offered the opinion that the Southern States Convention should not be transformed into a political caucus. "There seems to be a disposition," Quarles argued, "to force us into a political position," even though the great power of the convention lay in its nonpolitical significance. Any consideration of political questions would "weaken the moral force." However, to deny the majority of the delegates political expression at that time, as Quarles would have preferred, was impossible. Charges were flung against him of being "un-Republican." To that he replied quite indignantly: "There is a distinction between Republican principles and the Republican party. The Republican party may advocate Republican principles today and not tomorrow. I am opposed to pledging the colored people to any party. . . . Do these gentlemen here want me to pledge my people that they will not dissent simply because they come under the name of the Republican party? If they do, in the name of the people I represent, I enter my solemn protest." His anger now aroused, Quarles went on, fixing the difference between party and principle. "It is high time we commenced to think for ourselves," he explained, "to know when a party is right and its leaders are right. Do colored men create dissension in the Republican party? I say not."[39]

His outburst evoked much controversy. While several delegates agreed with Quarles' statements, some also felt, as did Frederick Douglass, that there was really no alternative to the Republican party. A Louisiana state legislator and delegate, John H. Burch, expressed the opinion that "this resolution can be easily arrived at. It pledges the support of the colored people to Republican principles, and the Republican

38. Ibid., p. 35; for Turner's career in the Georgia legislature, see E. Merton Coulter, *Negro Legislators in Georgia during the Reconstruction Period*, pp. 1–36.
39. Southern States Convention, *Proceedings*, pp. 36–37.

party. If it pledges the colored people to Republican principles, I for one, am willing, if they can find those principles alive in any other party, to go with them. If they can find them only in the Republican party, there I must stay."[40]

One of the issues stirred by this debate centered on the controversial belief that opposition to Grant and the regular Republicans equaled support of the Democrats. According to those who shared this sentiment, the Democrats would profit most from this division. One delegate even affirmed that "if my choice of candidates were circumscribed . . . or the nominee a man I would not select, yet if he were a Republican I would vote for him. It is the only way we can preserve our party and the liberties we enjoy."[41]

Others clearly disagreed. B. A. Bosemon of South Carolina maintained that "My complexion indicates that I must, of necessity, be a lover of [Republican] principles; that I must, of necessity, sustain them. But I am not bound, in consequence of that, to support the Republican party." Even Pinckney B. S. Pinchback, a stalwart Republican "from the very commencement of my life," was able to justify Quarles' argument. "That gentleman," Pinchback concluded, "said nothing that I know of that would render him liable to the charge of being anti-Republican."[42]

The controversy continued four days without a resolution. Several compromises were offered, but to no avail. One of the more extreme examples was that of Burch, who suggested a resolution that called for support of the party "in the same proportion" as the party had offered support to Negroes. Some favored it; others labeled it "ridiculous." It was tabled.[43] After other similar attempts to unravel the debate by compromise, Frederick Barbadoes of Washington, D. C., former executive secretary of the National Equal Rights League, proposed the following:

> Whereas this is a class Convention composed entirely of colored men, to consider their peculiar condition growing out of their enfranchisement, therefore be it—
> Resolved, That we deem it impolitic at this time to appear even to dictate or anticipate the action of the great Republican party, of which we form but a fraction.[44]

40. Ibid., p. 39.
41. Ibid., pp. 38–39.
42. Ibid., pp. 42–43.
43. Ibid., p. 44.
44. Ibid., p. 60.

Up to this point, Josiah Walls had been quiet during this debate as well as in other matters on the convention floor. He had been temporary chairman, but had not even addressed the delegates in that capacity. He was elected one of the several vice presidents of the convention, and he served on two of the permanent committees—those of outrages and of the address to the American public. Now, however, he rose to press his own view. To a pending resolution on the floor that supported Grant in limited fashion, Walls added an amendment: "that this Convention recommends to the next nominating Convention of the Republican party, the name of John Mercer Langston, as a candidate for the Vice Presidency of the United States."[45]

Because Walls at this point had opposed the regulars in his home county and state, one might have thought that this resolution, if it were made public, would have ended his career. And given the turmoil in South Carolina with the Klan, martial law, and conservative resentment of federal interference, his life seemingly would have been in jeopardy. His radical amendment was too much for the convention, but in the reaction to it, a compromise was reached. The delegates finally accepted a mild expression of support for Grant's second term.

Outside the convention there was some publicity, but not in Florida. Only the Tallahassee *Weekly Floridian*, the major conservative paper, commented on the meeting at all, and it erroneously reported that Barbadoes' resolution had been accepted.[46] It was another matter elsewhere. Upon noting Walls' nomination of a black man to such high office, the *Washington Daily Morning Chronicle* editorialized: "We have among us several men of prominence who demand the nomination and election of colored men as such, and because of their race, and demand that all colored men shall act with them. In doing so they deny a fundamental Republican principle."[47] Frederick Douglass retorted sarcastically a few days later: "We have among us [white Republicans] . . . who tell the colored Republicans not to nominate a colored man to office, as it will drive white Republicans from the party, and through this sort of intimidation have in many instances prevented the representation of colored men in the Legislature, as that white Republican who would refuse to vote for a colored Republican has that in him which prevents him from being able to represent fairly his black brother."[48]

45. Ibid., p. 63.
46. October 15, 1871.
47. October 23, 1871.
48. (Washington) *New National Era*, October 26, 1871.

Walls was accused of leaving South Carolina and, upon his return to Washington, of asking President Grant to declare martial law in Leon and several adjoining Florida counties.[49] He replied with a sweeping denial of the charge: "I unhesitatingly denounce the article referred to . . . as a malicious falsehood. Never have I mentioned Leon County to the President, nor has anyone attempted to 'induce' me to do so."[50] What he had done was to cheer wholeheartedly for Grant's action in South Carolina. As chairman of the convention's committee on outrages, Walls' report to the delegates condemned the Klan for its "sole purpose of intimidating the colored people in the exercise of their rights as citizens of the United States." It also attacked "those who have the power to enforce the law [but who] have acted in sympathy with the Klan by countenancing their disloyalty, and not bringing said parties to trial."[51]

Walls did not escape all political repercussions for his resolution or his independent nature. At the April 1872 meeting of the Florida Republican executive committee, of which Henry Harmon was a member, Dennis Eagan of Madison, F. T. Wicker of Key West, John W. Butler of Milton, J. M. Armstrong of Lake City, Hiram Potter of Pensacola, and Walls were chosen as Florida's delegation to the national Republican convention that met in Philadelphia in June.[52] Of course Grant was easily renominated, and the Florida delegation had ironclad instructions to support only the incumbent. However, during the convention the national executive committee was reported to have demanded a meeting with the rebellious Florida congressman specifically to ascertain his loyalty. Walls issued "an unequivocal denial" to all charges that he opposed Grant's renomination.[53]

In later years, Frederick Douglass reflected on the depth of the black disaffection with Grantism and regular Republicanism in this period. He himself had remained firmly loyal to the President, and in April 1872, at a meeting of the National Negro Convention in New Orleans, he continued to exert enough influence to win support for the president's second-term bid. At that convention, Douglass was chosen chairman in honor of his efforts on behalf of his race. Alonzo Ransier, presiding as temporary chairman, remarked that it was fitting for Douglass to "pre-

49. (Tallahassee) *Weekly Floridian*, December 5, 1871.
50. Ibid., December 19, 1871.
51. Southern States Convention, *Proceedings*, p. 64.
52. William Purman to Chandler, April 25, 1872, Chandler Papers, vol. 21.
53. *Washington Star*, June 4, 1872, quoted in *Tallahassee Sentinel*, June 15, 1872.

side over the assembled representatives of those who love and honor him."[54]

As no detailed record remains of the proceedings, it is not known if Walls attended. However, there must have been others who were critical of the party, for only with great effort was Douglass able to persuade the convention to pledge to Grant and the party "unwavering devotion." Douglass, in his autobiography, recalled his efforts to quell dissent in New Orleans: "The division in the Republican ranks seemed to be growing deeper and broader every day. The colored people of the country were much affected by the threatened disruption, and their leaders were much divided as to the side upon which they should give their voice and vote . . . and there was in the convention . . . a strong disposition to fraternize with the new party. . . . Against this policy I exerted whatever influence I possessed, and I think, succeeded in holding back that convention from . . . a fatal political blunder."[55]

The following year, in early December, the largest of the National Negro Conventions of the Reconstruction period met in Washington, D.C. It was called for "the special purpose of impressing on Congress the absolute necessity of passing a Civil Rights Bill."[56] By this time, civil rights superseded most other questions for the black people. The previous Congresses had failed to produce meaningful legislation, and the convention hoped to convince the legislators that such a bill, most notably Charles Sumner's supplementary civil rights bill, was necessary. To George Downing, this need was "paramount to other questions."[57]

In Congress at the time, Walls joined other Negro leaders for the meeting. He nominated Pinchback, who was accepted by acclamation, for chairman; he also served on the committee of permanent organization.[58] There were some 200 to 300 delegates present when the meeting settled down to business on December 9, 1873. Pinchback's inaugural speech expanded on the purpose of the gathering: "The members of the convention now ask the National Legislature to give them such privileges as are accorded to the white race. These embrace the rights of admission into public schools, theatres, hotels, and on steamboats, and on railroad cars. It is a fallacy to say that the colored race are

54. (Washington) *New National Era*, May 2, 1872.
55. *Life and Times of Frederick Douglass*, pp. 415–16.
56. (Washington) *New National Era*, October 23, 1873; see also the call and constitution of the National Civil Rights Association in Chandler Papers, vol. 27.
57. (Washington) *New National Era*, November 4, 1873.
58. Ibid., December 11, 1873.

slaves by instinct. They were free before they were seized by their former captors and traders, and a long series of years of bondage has not extinguished their love of freedom." One interesting sidelight to Pinchback's references to public discrimination was opened by a delegate from Virginia named Medford who castigated the black barbers and saloon-keepers of Washington. It was his opinion that these men "were unwilling to award fellow colored men equal rights." Some of the Negro merchants had large white clienteles, which they feared losing if blacks were admitted to their establishments.[59]

As the primary purpose of the meeting was to lobby for a specific bill, several of the delegations fanned out to garner support. For example, the New York delegates visited their congressional representatives; on December 10, New York senators Roscoe Conkling and Reuben Fenton both pledged to vote for the bill, and on the next day, the New York members of the House made similar pledges.[60]

Two separate visits were made to President Grant. The first visit was to the White House on December 10 and present were the Louisiana representatives to the convention, headed by James Lewis and Pinchback. In a brief and cordial meeting, the president expressed his opinion that although Negroes were as yet still dispossessed of certain rights, Congress was sure to pass "some civil rights bill" in the present session. However, Grant gave warning to his visitors that if such a bill were not forthcoming, it would be a result of some "extreme measure" urged by purported friends of Negroes. The second meeting with Grant resulted in his repeating his earlier view. To the group of delegates, headed by George Downing, that met with him on December 12, Grant added that despite the probable passage of a civil rights measure, the Negro people should continue to be aware of the "prejudice existing against them."[61]

The convention adjourned on December 14, 1873, after drafting a memorial to the public. In it one can easily note the change in sentiment. It pointed out that the Democratic platform equaled the Republican one on civil rights and it emphasized the failure of the Republican commitment to equality.[62] The next day, the *New York Times* summarized the results of the meeting: "Little good was done by the National Civil Rights Association during its late session. The demand for passage of Mr. Sumner's bill is placed among the leading results of the meeting, and

---

59. *New York Times*, December 10–12, 1873.
60. Ibid., December 12, 1873.
61. Ibid., December 11, 13, 1873.
62. U. S. Congress, 43d Cong., 1st sess., *House Miscellaneous Document 44*.

that such an issue should have been considered of paramount importance is not encouraging. It is time for the leaders of the colored race to turn their attention to the material condition of their followers. The negroes are practically on the same footing with other citizens, and they should now be made to understand that the future depends entirely upon their own industry and frugality."[63]

The National Negro Convention movement ground to a halt in 1873, in part because the leaders realized that no further advancement could be made through legislation. The battle for rights had been won in the sense that the acts were now laws; but, for the most part, the black leaders understood their defeat. Equal rights were still denied to black people, and the civil rights law which eventually passed was a virtual dead letter. Moreover, the general depression in that year, affecting white and black Americans alike, contributed to a turning away from racial-political issues. Yet, black organizations and black disaffection with their status in American society did not end here. In 1875, Isaac Myers established the Colored Men's Progressive and Cooperative Union, and the first convention of Negro newspapermen met in Cincinnati. Similar activity continued in the post-Reconstruction period. The Young Men's Progressive Association was formed in New Orleans in 1878, while the Civil Rights Congress and the Mutual United Brotherhood of Liberty of the United States were established in 1883. Both the founders' conventions of the Afro-American League and the Convention of Colored Americans occurred in 1890. Thus, although the National Negro Convention in Reconstruction failed to produce meaningful change for Negroes, the black organizations that followed bear witness to its legacy and that of the men, like Josiah Walls, who participated in it.

63. December 15, 1873.

7

On the Other Side of the
Senate, 1876–1879

W ALLS did not leave Washington immediately after losing his congressional seat to J. J. Finley on March 29, 1876. In addition to the normal procedure of packing personal belongings, saying good-bye to friends and acquaintances, and closing his office, he remained for the ceremony dedicating the freedmen's memorial statue of Abraham Lincoln on April 14. Costing more than $17,000, which had been raised by contributions from Negroes throughout the country, the project had been initiated by Charlotte Scott of Marietta, Ohio, who in the first days after the tragic assassination began to collect money to build the memorial. Walls and John Mercer Langston cosigned the public invitation to the unveiling. April 14 was declared a government holiday in Washington, and the president, members of both houses of Congress, the justices of the Supreme Court, and other government officials witnessed a large procession of Negroes to Lincoln Park.[1]

There Frederick Douglass read the Emancipation Proclamation and delivered an oration. His speech provided clear evidence that even in death Lincoln had not been the idol of the Negro race: "It must be admitted . . . even here in the presence of the monument we have erected to his memory, that [Lincoln] was not, in the fullest sense of the word,

1. (Jacksonville) *Florida Union*, April 20, 1876. The statue was designed by Thomas Bailey to attract visitors to newly planted Lincoln Park, which had been laid out in early 1871 at what was then the end of East Capitol Street. See Constance McLaughlin Green, *Washington: Village and Capitol, 1800–1878*, pp. 347, 398. An account of the proceedings can be found in Frederick Douglass, *Oration by Frederick Douglass Delivered on the Occasion of the Unveiling of the Freedmen's Monument in Memory of Abraham Lincoln in Lincoln Park, Washington, D.C., April 14, 1876*, passim.

either our man or our model. In his interests, in his associations, in his habits of thought and in his prejudices, he was a white man. . . . He was preeminently the white man's President, entirely devoted to the welfare of white men. . . . We are at best his step-children, children by adoption, children by force of circumstances and necessity." The reason for the memorial, Douglass explained, was so that when "it shall be said that the colored man is soulless, that he has no appreciation of benefits or benefactors—when the foul reproach of ingratitude is hurled . . . we may calmly point to the monument we have this day erected to the memory of Abraham Lincoln."[2] Grant himself then drew back the covering over the twelve-foot-high bronze figure of the Great Emancipator atop its ten-foot-high pedestal. This ceremony was Josiah Walls' last public function in Washington.

Although he was no longer a congressman, his political options were not closed. Reportedly President Grant offered him a federal appointment to the postmastership at Key West. Walls apparently refused, preferring to make still another try for office.[3] At least one Florida newspaper considered him a force to be reckoned with in the state, remarking that as a result of Finley, the pertinent question now to be asked is "Where is Walls?—in our State politics." The paper offered a clue: "We understand he desires to run on the Republican State ticket as Lieutenant-Governor. The party might do worse, for Mr. Walls is not the worst man in politics in the State, while he is not qualified for a Representative in Congress."[4] Upon his return to Alachua County, however, he discovered that once more Leonard Dennis had assumed control of the local Republican party organization. Before reaching for any higher office, again Walls had to reassert his leadership on the local level.

He began in the same fashion that had proved successful in the past. Disavowing any intent to divide Alachua County Republicans on factional or racial lines, he attacked the white Republicans for their false loyalties. The party under Dennis had already met to select the delegates for the Republican state nominating convention that was to be held on May 31, in Madison.[5] The local meeting had been held on April 13 at Roper's Hall in Gainesville. Neither Walls, who as yet had not returned

2. Douglass, *Life and Times of Frederick Douglass*, pp. 481–93.
3. (Jacksonville) *Florida Union*, May 8, 1876; (Jacksonville) *Florida Sun*, May 9, 1876.
4. *Florida Sun*, March 11, 1876.
5. The date and setting for the statewide meeting had been set at the Republican State Central Committee meeting at Live Oak on April 7, 1876.

from Washington, nor any of his known supporters, was chosen for the Alachua slate. The black editor of Gainesville's *Florida Sentinel*, Mathew M. Lewey, did attend the meeting. Lewey, a Walls supporter, explained that the Dennis-led group represented no more than 75 or 80 of the some 1,600 Republican voters in the county. He also described how the "Little Giant" had ordered the speaker's platform torn down at a mass rally on April 18 after a Walls Republican had tried to address the crowd. Dennis defended his action on the grounds that the wooden platform was "private property."[6] For this particular rally, the "Little Giant" had public notices printed and circulated throughout the county. These circulars, which were posted on pine trees at every crossroad, announced that "the best Republican speakers" in the state would be in attendance. One disgruntled resident, however, wrote that the real purpose of the meeting was "to induce our fellow citizens to endorse or ratify certain delegates who were appointed at a so-called convention at Roper's Hall."[7]

In the meantime, even before their leader's return to Gainesville, the Walls faction had begun to fight back. On the evening of March 9, 1876, a pro-Walls Republican rally took place at the Union Academy. J. Willis Menard, who at one time in the past had challenged Walls' leadership of East Florida Negroes, attacked the Dennis faction. Menard castigated them for being good Republicans only "when the party served their selfish purposes, and that when it did not . . . they were ready and willing to hand the colored troops over to the tender mercies of the Democrats."[8]

One of the clearer issues between the factions in this local split was the choice for governor. The leading candidates were Gov. Marcellus Stearns, the incumbent, and Sen. Simon B. Conover. The regulars supported Stearns. At the Union Academy meeting, however, the governor came in for heavy criticism from Theodore Gass, another Walls supporter who chaired the meeting in Walls' absence.

Shortly after he arrived in the county, Walls, as chairman of the county Republican executive committee, ordered a second meeting. At this gathering on April 29, he declared that all the previous efforts of Dennis and his faction were illegal. He typed the forthcoming Madison convention of Florida Republicans "a fraud" and refused to support either Stearns or Conover. Instead, Walls drew together an independent delegation to contest the Dennis-contrived slate at the statewide

6. (Jacksonville) *Florida Sun*, May 27, 1876.
7. Ibid., May 23, 1876.
8. Ibid., March 11, 1876.

convention.[9] One observer of the Union Academy meeting commented on the "general indignation" at the fact that Finley had won the contested congressional seat for the district, and went on to note that the gathering "had more the appearance of a mass meeting, than a delegated body, and yet it was convened under the ordinary call of the County Executive Committee." He also registered surprise that no newspaper in the state covered it despite the fact that "it was the largest ever held in the county."[10]

When the state nominating convention did meet in Madison on May 31 to select the nominee for governor, both Alachua factions were present. The committee on credentials had to decide which delegation to seat. It is of interest, although decidedly puzzling, to note that William K. Cessna, no warm advocate of Walls in the past, was a member of both delegations.[11] The Alachua County Republicans were not the only local party organization which was split at this time. Six other counties also sent competing delegations to the Madison convention.[12]

The committee on credentials allowed both Walls and Dennis to present their cases. Dennis' appearance was "clear, methodical, decided, and [he] had his papers in order." On the other hand, although also allotted twenty minutes to present his side of the matter, Walls did not pursue it wholeheartedly: "Walls said but little, not even contradicting Dennis's version of the meeting."[13] The Dennis Republicans were seated; however, in a conciliatory gesture Dennis moved that Walls be invited to take a seat as a guest of the convention.[14]

Walls' peculiar behavior in all of this requires examination. At some point between his return to Florida in late April and the Madison convention on May 31, he had decided to back Conover despite his earlier independent position, as Stearns had managed to sew up the renomination even before the meeting took place. Stearns supposedly had gathered his forces at a preconvention caucus in Jacksonville, thereby cutting off Conover from any support of the regular

9. (Jacksonville) *Florida Union*, May 3, 1876.

10. (Jacksonville) *Florida Sun*, May 9, 1876.

11. The Walls delegation included George Arnow, John Brown, Cessna, T. C. Gass, S. F. Halliday, Mathew Lewey, Watson Porter, and George Washington. The Dennis delegation included Sheriff L. A. Barnes, R. H. Black, Paul Brown, Cessna, Joe Rowe, Isaac St. Clair, Joseph Valentine, and Thomas Vance.

12. Davis, *Civil War and Reconstruction in Florida*, p. 690; *Tallahassee Sentinel*, June 3, 1876; (Jacksonville) *Florida Union*, June 13, 1876.

13. (Jacksonville) *Florida Sun*, June 3, 1876.

14. *Tallahassee Sentinel*, June 3, 1876.

Republicans.[15] Walls, having decided not to fight for the convention seat he had already lost to Dennis, decided instead to attend the factional convention in which Conover would be nominated. The only other possible explanation for his weak effort to gain the Alachua County credentials at Madison was that he and Dennis secretly had reached some sort of understanding between themselves, but events in the coming short space of time proved that not to have been the case. There is no indication that Walls and Dennis made peace before the summer of 1876.

Immediately following the formal nomination of Stearns, several dissenters who supported Conover assembled in a "bolters' convention," also in Madison. Walls was chosen honorary chairman of the new Republican meeting. Conover was nominated for governor, and Joseph Lee, a Negro from Sumter County, was selected to be his running mate. Walls, Sherman Conant, William Purman (thus casting at least some doubt on his part in Walls' unseating), Alva Knight, John Scott, and J. Willis Menard, along with F. E. Grossman and J. B. Stickney, formed the Conover campaign committee.[16] At a Jacksonville meeting on June 29, 1876, they drew up plans to form a statewide committee around Conover and Lee and resolved to meet twice per month until the election.[17]

During July, appeals for party unity grew. Even another Republican nominating convention was suggested, and William Gleason, the first lieutenant governor of Florida after the Civil War, was put forth as a gubernatorial compromise choice.[18] "J. T. S." wrote from East Florida that the party had better heal its differences before "every right and privilege of [the Negro] race are endangered."[19] In Alachua County, Dennis replied to a letter from A. G. Whitfield, who pleaded that the competition between the Republican factions must cease. To Whitfield's suggestion that a mass meeting be held to rally all sides, the "Little Giant" answered: "In regard to the expediency of calling a mass meeting for the purpose of endorsement of either of the two candidates for Governor, you must be the judge. I consider it expedient to work for the election of M. L. Stearns . . . until some proof can be shown that he is not entitled to my vote. . . . I shall do all I can to cause his election, and if a

15. Davis, *Civil War and Reconstruction in Florida*, pp. 689–90.
16. *Tallahassee Sentinel*, June 8, 1876.
17. (Jacksonville) *Florida Sun*, July 1, 1876.
18. John H. Fry to William Gleason, July 20, 1876, William Gleason Papers. Gleason had just returned from Europe and was head of the Republican State Central Committee.
19. (Jacksonville) *Florida Union*, July 27, 1876.

faction calling themselves Republicans are determined to adhere to their bolting candidate, and by doing so turn the State over to the Democrats, they alone must bear the responsibility."[20]

As the pressure mounted, the Conover faction was forced back into the regular fold. The national Republican executive committee, meeting in New York City in early August, turned down the senator's request that he, not Stearns, be recognized as the legitimate Republican candidate.[21] John Rollins of Duval County wrote Senator Chandler of the national committee that "if the Republicans hold to natural law, to maintain the rights of all regardless of race or color," they should be able to win. He added, however, that "the only exception will be perhaps that the negroes will not hold quite so many offices which to *every decent* man north or south should be considered an end to be worked and prayed for."[22] On September 5, 1876, the Conover bid was at an end. The senator published a statement of his withdrawal and in turn endorsed the regular Republican candidates.[23]

Walls followed suit. Earlier, at the Alachua County district convention, he won the nomination for state senator by acclamation, although he had announced at the time that he was behind Conover and opposed to Stearns and Dennis.[24] On July 6, 1876, the *Gainesville Times* discussed the Walls-Dennis feud at length:

> Ex-Congressman Walls has taken time by the forelock and entered the field for the State Senate in this District. His haste evinces his desire to get a good running start of "Little Dennis," whose tactics and strength he by no means despises. Walls has all along avowed a determination to divest his pugnacious and capricious adversary of his unlimited and abused political power. In this he certainly has the approval of the best men in the Republican party.
>
> Those on whom [Dennis] has conferred the honors and pickings of office, seem disposed to prop up his weakening political underpinning; and he, and his friends, altogether, will make Walls's pathway to Senatorial honors a fatiguing and thorny one. But it is surmised by some that there will be a cordial "making-up" between the Walls and Dennis factions before the end of the political campaign. The discordant elements of the Republican party have

20. Ibid., July 18, 1876.
21. *Tallahassee Sentinel*, August 5, 1876.
22. (Jacksonville) *Florida Union*, September 6, 1876.
23. John F. Rollins to Chandler, August 9, 1876, Chandler Papers, vol. 42.
24. (Jacksonville) *Florida Sun*, June 13, 1876.

always exhibited a weakness in that direction. . . . But, in that event, which one, Walls or Dennis, will receive the honor of being the sole choice of the Republicans of this District?

Their particular feud had ended even before Conover pulled out in September. The first step toward peace between the local factions came at a meeting of the Hayes-Wheeler Club in Gainesville on the night of August 7, 1876. To avoid a fight at the meeting, William K. Cessna was elected president; one Walls supporter, Theodore Gass, and one Dennis supporter, Sheriff L. A. Barnes, were the vice presidents. Dennis and Walls contented themselves with serving on the registration committee. By doing so, they equally supervised who, and how many, of each faction were enrolled as members. It was reported that both men had decided to settle their differences, and they declared in separate speeches that all past disagreements "as individuals, or as representatives of different factions, were settled, and that they were now thoroughly and heartily united." A local convention to select the delegates to the congressional convention in Jacksonville was agreed upon. As the meeting ended one reporter commented on the new harmony: "This is the beginning of the end of all differences in the Republican ranks in 'old Alachua,' assures a '68 majority to the party in '76, which means, 'Lie down Tilden, and let Hayes pass over.' "[25]

The Republican nominating convention for the second congressional district in East Florida was held in Jacksonville on August 15, and Walls hoped to win a fourth bid. Going into the meeting, Walls' strength was difficult to assess. He had been unable to defeat Dennis through power politics or by independence. Unlike 1874, this time Walls and not the "Little Giant" had been forced to compromise. On the other hand, he already had secured the nomination to the state senate from the thirteenth district, and he also had reached a working truce with Dennis and the regulars. In Jacksonville he confessed that while he would enjoy a fourth nomination to Congress, he had no hopes of achieving it. Yet he was appointed to the district executive committee, and Henry Harmon was elected chairman of the convention when Sherman Conant decided not to contest the honor.[26]

Walls' most severe problem was his relationship with Stearns. He was accused by blacks of having "sold-out" to the regular faction and of abandoning Conover. While the evidence indicates that Walls and Dennis

25. (Jacksonville) *Florida Union*, August 11, 12, 1876.
26. *Tallahassee Sentinel*, August 19, 1876.

had made their peace prior to the withdrawal of Conover from the gubernatorial race, it is not known whether Walls actually received money to swing over to the other side. John Wallace accused Stearns of offering, and Conover of accepting, $1,200 to $1,500 to end the factionalism and his independent campaign.[27] Walls argued in Jacksonville that his only sellout was to the platform resolutions and to the regular candidates.[28]

After the first informal ballot it was clear that Walls was still a force to be reckoned with. He had received fifteen votes; Negro John Scott had gotten nineteen; Dennis Eagan had totaled twelve; and Horatio Bisbee, district attorney from Duval County and a leader of the regulars in East Florida, had garnered seven. At the conclusion of two more informal and five more formal ballots, the four men still were deadlocked. On the next vote the Duval County delegation, which had been behind Scott, switched to Bisbee. With that turn he was nominated easily.[29] For Walls the vote marked the end of his effort at regaining his congressional seat within the regular Republican ranks. He congratulated the victor and pledged to work for Bisbee's election against the incumbent Finley.

Returning home, Walls spent much of his time working for the party's nominees. He had little to fear from his conservative opponent for the state senate, Thomas F. King, a judge in Levy County. King had been nominated by acclamation at a Democratic district convention on August 10. The first ballot had given him over two-thirds of the total, and after his nomination he pledged to support the Democratic party.[30] At this point, however, Alachua County still had a Republican majority, and Walls' victory was assured. Both he and Dennis continued the Hayes-Wheeler club meetings. At a meeting on the evening of August 21, 1876, at the Union Academy in Gainesville, conservative Democrat James B. Brown, a "wealthy . . . Bourbon of the first water," addressed the club on the financial condition of the country. Brown had been invited by some of the Negro members, but Dennis refused to admit him. Walls, however, won a motion to allow Brown the floor over the "Little Giant's" objections. In turn Dennis' motion also passed forbidding Brown to address the members for more than twenty minutes. When Brown finished, Dennis rose to reply to his charges that Republicans had squandered the wealth of Alachua County's taxpayers. While

27. *Carpetbag Rule in Florida*, p. 333.
28. *Tallahassee Sentinel*, August 19, 1876.
29. Ibid.
30. (Tallahassee) *Weekly Floridian*, August 22, 1876.

he was countering Brown, "a shot was fired from a gun or a pistol through the window directly in front of Mr. Dennis. Almost simultaneously with this, another shot was fired through a side window." No one was hurt, and the meeting resumed. This incident was one of the few recorded in Alachua County during an otherwise peaceful campaign. Indeed, a short time later Walls was invited to, and addressed, the Tilden-Hendricks club in Gainesville.[31]

The election was held on November 7, 1876, and as expected Walls won his race against King with ease, the vote being 2,280 to 1,734.[32] The vote totals in the county were crucial for the major Republican candidates including, of course, the presidential contestants. Walls himself played only a minor role in the alleged frauds during the days after the election. According to the Democrats, the central issue in Alachua County was the illegal addition of 219 extra votes for the opposition slate into the Archer second precinct ballot box. The alleged culprits were the election officials stationed there, Green Moore, Thomas Vance, and Richard Black. They reputedly helped Leonard Dennis stuff the box which had been taken to his Gainesville home on election night.[33]

None of the national committees which investigated implicated Walls—neither the House and Senate committees working on the presidential race between Rutherford Hayes and Samuel Tilden nor the House committee on contested elections in charge of the congressional race between Horatio Bisbee and J. J. Finley. However, Floyd Dukes, the Democratic election inspector at the Archer precinct and one of the few conservative blacks in the district, charged before each of the committees that Walls had attempted to bribe him into swearing by affidavit that the Republican total was 399 rather than 180 votes. Dukes stated that on the morning of November 25, at approximately 8:00 A.M., Walls and William Belton, Alachua County justice of the peace, drove to his farm near Archer. Dukes alleged that he was offered $25 by Walls for his signature on the affidavit in question. When he refused to sign, Belton, who had waited in the buggy while the two men talked for fifteen minutes in Dukes' wagon shed, tried also to get his signature. Dukes steadfastly opposed signing anything, however, and the two visitors left, breakfasted in Archer, separated to conduct private business, and then

31. *Tallahassee Sentinel*, September 2, 1876; (Jacksonville) *Florida Union*, August 25, 1876; U. S. Congress, 44th Cong., 2d sess., *Senate Report 611*, part 2, pp. 201–5.

32. *Senate Report 611*, part 2, p. 225. Walls won in Alachua County, and Thomas King carried the much less heavily populated Levy County in the election in the thirteenth district.

33. Jerrell H. Shofner, "Fraud and Intimidation in the Florida Election of 1876."

met again on the train back to Gainesville that evening. At that point Belton had a signature, apparently Dukes', on the affidavit.[34]

Both Walls and Belton testified before the senate committee, and the latter also testified before the House committee on contested elections. In the latter instance, Congressman Finley's attorney inquired further about the details of the meeting at Dukes' farm. Belton confirmed that he and Walls had left Gainesville for Archer before daylight on November 25, 1876, a dark and rainy morning, in a two-horse buggy hired by Walls. Pressed by the attorney's efforts to discredit Republican testimony, Belton also admitted that a bottle of whiskey had been consumed on the journey, although he had had but one or two drinks. Upon reaching Archer, Walls inquired as to the whereabouts of Dukes, and then asked for directions to the farm after learning the man was not in town. Belton testified further that he acquired the signature at the farm and left for town. He also added that Walls had paid him mileage for the trip, about $3, and that the entire affair had been arranged at a meeting of Walls, Dennis, himself, and others at the Gainesville courthouse three days earlier.[35]

Walls' testimony partly corroborated that of Belton, and was in direct conflict with Dukes' version. Walls swore before the senate investigators that he had never offered Dukes a bribe for his signature. When the conservative refused to sign freely, Walls returned to Archer, breakfasted on "a plate of oysters," and witnessed Belton and Dukes entering an office together. He stated he never saw the actual signing of the document. Moreover, he explained that his primary purpose in going to Archer to see Dukes had no connection with politics, but rather had been on business: "There had been a case here in court in which [Dukes'] son-in-law . . . was killed by another man, and the case came before the grand jury and a true bill was not found; of course, the young man was not brought before the court. I was defending this young man. I understood that Mr. Dukes had very harsh feelings towards myself because he thought I used my influence—certain influences—to keep this true bill from being read . . . and I wished to give him an explanation. . . . I made mention of that to him that morning; and immediately after speaking to him about that, I asked him about the affidavit and then he said no, and there was no other question between him and me."[36]

34. U. S. Congress, 45th Cong., 1st sess., "Papers in the Case of Finley vs. Bisbee, Second Congressional District of Florida," *House Miscellaneous Document 10*, pp. 112–15.
35. Ibid., pp. 126–32, 352–55.
36. U. S. Congress, 44th Cong., 2d sess., "Testimony Taken before the Special

Beyond this instance, Walls apparently was uninvolved in the disputed election. On the day of the voting he had stayed in Gainesville, and Thomas Vance was sent to observe the Archer polling. Moreover, Walls was never indicted as being present at Dennis' house on the night the ballots allegedly were stuffed.

There were no reported cases of election-day violence in Alachua County, although a small detachment of United States troops had been moved from Tampa to Gainesville to prevent trouble at the polls. One resident described the tense situation that existed among white Democrats during the few days afterwards. Writing to his brother Edward on November 11, Edwin L'Engle took note of "the greatest excitement [that] has prevailed since the elections. The negroes are desperate and dangerous to the peace of our community. Much anxiety has been felt about the town being burnt by the negroes. Some 400 armed negroes were in the suburbs of the town last night and [there were] rumors that it was their intention to fire the town. We have the whiskey shops closed and a heavy force of police on duty and six men at a time watching the clerk's office to prevent any alterations of the ballots or returns. The radical majority . . . may be reduced by throwing out boxes on account of fraud."[37]

A postscript on this election occurred in 1882, when a Negro, Jacob Hawkins, member of the Alachua County election board of canvassers in 1876, spent the night at the Kansas farm of one John Detwiler. Detwiler reported that Hawkins admitted to him that Tilden had in fact polled the most votes in Alachua County.[38] Historians have tended to agree. Most argue that a "fair" count insured a Democratic victory, while a "free" election would have carried for the Republicans and Hayes.[39]

During this same period Walls also served as a member of the Alachua County board of commissioners, to which he had been appointed in October 1876. The records of the commission meetings are sparse, stating in most entries no more than the times of the meetings and the members present. However, it is known that he served with Paul Brown, Dennis, Henry James (not related to Garth), and Irving Webster, the county clerk and auditor. Walls was appointed or elected presi-

---

Committee on Investigation of the Election in Florida, Appointed under Resolution of the House of Representatives, Forty-fourth Congress, December 4, 1876," *House Miscellaneous Document 35*, part 1, pp. 221–24.

37. November 5, 1876, L'Engle Papers, mss. box 5, folder 85.

38. John Y. Detwiler narrative relative to the Presidential Election of 1876 in Florida.

39. Record Book A, Clerk of the Circuit Court, Alachua County Courthouse.

dent pro tem of the county commission on December 11, 1876, and he served in that capacity throughout most of the month of January 1877.[40]

While thus engaged, he also entered the state senate on January 2, 1877. Promptly at twelve noon on that day, he handed his election certificate to the clerk of the senate and was sworn in as the representative from the thirteenth district. The situation was markedly different from that of 1869–70 when he first had entered the state legislature. Then, the Republicans were the ascendant political power. Now, they were consigned only to harassing the Democratic majority, and wielding effective power was out of the question.

For the few blacks left in the senate and the assembly, things were even worse. Their political leverage had all but disappeared. Despite repeated assertions that the Democrats would prove their goodwill toward the Negro race, most southern Negroes would have agreed with Rev. Alexander Crummell's remark concerning Frederick Douglass' appointment as minister to Haiti: "I have the most serious misgivings, for President Hayes putting one black man forward does not compensate for his putting back 4½ million black men in the south, and giving supremacy . . . to the old power-holding body."[41]

Walls' first day in the senate amply illustrated the weakness of the Republican position. The Democrats selected the senate officers and the officials, from secretary to doorkeeper and janitor. Walls and his fellow Republicans always voted in the minority. It must have surprised even Walls when his choice for senate chaplain, E. D. Many, was elected. Walls did sponsor a motion designed to promote some Republican leverage. It called for the standing committees in the senate to be elected by a two-thirds vote rather than appointed by the president. This would have given the Republicans veto power over the Democratic choices, but the motion lost heavily. As a result of his disgust with the situation, Walls did not show up for the afternoon session on that first day of business.[42] On the second day of the regular session, he found he had been appointed to five committees (none of which he chaired): education, public lands, militia, fisheries, and state affairs. The follow-

40. Shofner, "Fraud and Intimidation in the Florida Election of 1876," passim; for other secondary studies on the particular election see also C. Vann Woodward, *Reunion and Reaction*, and Albert M. Gibson, *A Political Crime: The History of the Great Fraud.*

41. Crummell to J. W. Cromwell, April 25, 1877, Alexander Crummell Papers.

42. *Senate Journal. A Journal of the Proceedings of the Senate of the State of Florida at the Ninth Session of the Legislature, Begun . . . January 2, 1877*, pp. 3–10.

ing day, Walls tried to resign from all but the committee on education, but he was refused.[43]

The only resolution in the senate that session which would have had a beneficial effect upon Negroes was sponsored by Walls on January 10. He asked that his committee on education be empowered to "examine the manner in which the Public Schools have been conducted in the several counties."[44] This was agreed to. However, he was alone among the members of his committee in favoring a bill that would have made public education mandatory for all Florida children between the ages of six and fifteen. The bill had been worded without reference to race in the hope that the omission might help its passage. The minority report was signed only by Walls, and it urged the enactment of this legislation because "the moral, social, and political prosperity of our State depends more on the education of the youth than on anything else."[45] The vote came on February 2, and the result was 19 to 2 against the measure. John Wallace and Walls were its only proponents.[46]

The session ended in March, and there is no indication that Walls remained in Tallahassee any longer. It is likely that he returned in July for a statewide Negro convention, although he was not reported to have made an address. Henry Harmon and Mathew Lewey were there as the regular delegates from Alachua County. The conservative *Jacksonville Daily Sun and Press* viewed the July 4 Negro convention with some distrust, noting especially that several leading white Republicans were to attend. "These astute gentlemen see the drift of sentiment among the colored people, and deem it wise to seek its control rather than oppose it." The paper predicted another "new departure" effort.[47]

Actually only Senator Conover addressed the gathering, and he advised the Negroes of Florida to remain quiet and uncritical, at least publicly. He did add that "I do not meantime wish to be understood as advising that you should altogether withdraw your interest in politics." The members of the convention apparently did not make public their recriminations about their present political situation. There was little they could do to alter it. The *Tallahassee Weekly Floridian* commented: "On the whole we are inclined to applaud . . . the Convention for [its] good sense. They make no foolish complainings and raise no groundless

43. Ibid., p. 20.
44. Ibid., p. 32.
45. Ibid., p. 173.
46. Ibid., p. 181.
47. June 30, 1877.

fears. They did not get much into politics and have fairly presented their material wants and needs."[48] Following the drafting of a memorial to the people of the state, the meeting adjourned.

In the next session of the senate, convened on January 7, 1879, Walls heeded Conover's unexpressed advice to withdraw from politics. His role in the legislature narrowed further. On his own motion, he, W. B. Barnes of the third district (Jackson County), and Silas Niblack, now in the state senate from the fourteenth district, formed the honorary committee to "attend" Governor Drew and inform him that the senate was duly organized and awaiting his message. Thus, in his last session Walls repeated his first official act as a state legislator in 1869. He was appointed to only three committees as a holdover senator: printing, state affairs, and militia.[49]

Early in this session he twice sponsored motions asking that the state legislature adjourn in time for the members to attend the state fair in Gainesville, scheduled to open on February 25. The first effort resulted in his motion being laid on the table, and on its second try it was defeated soundly.[50] Also during this session the two houses convened in joint assembly to elect the United States senator who would succeed Simon B. Conover in March. It was, of course, a foregone conclusion that the Democrats would nominate whomever they pleased, and Wilkinson Call won handily. However, it is interesting to note that now that it was of no consequence, Dennis and Walls paid their compliments to each other. Walls nominated Dennis in the senate; the latter received only his colleague's one vote. In the assembly Dennis nominated Walls, who then received his single vote from the "Little Giant."[51] The other Republicans in both houses also refrained from supporting the Democratic choice, casting their votes instead for Conover. The *Floridian*, in congratulating Call, took note of this unnecessary Republican partisanship: "We congratulate the Democracy on the fact that the Senator elected will go to Washington owing his election solely to the party for whose success he has labored so earnestly. He received no Republican vote in the election. . . . Perhaps this was natural, but it would have been a graceful act had some of the Republican members given him their support instead of

---

48. July 10, 1877.
49. *Senate Journal. A Journal of the Proceedings of the Senate of the State of Florida at the Tenth Session of the Legislature, Begun . . . January 7, 1879*, pp. 5, 6–8.
50. Ibid., pp. 42, 47–48.
51. Ibid., pp. 75–76; *Assembly Journal. A Journal of the Proceedings of the Assembly of the State of Florida, at its Tenth Session, Begun . . . January 7, 1879*, pp. 51–52.

throwing their votes away in meaningless compliment to others."[52]

Two weeks later, February 25, 1879, Walls was granted an indefinite leave of absence from the senate. His avowed reason was "sickness in the family."[53] He returned two days later to answer the Friday afternoon roll call, which proved to be his last.[54] Indeed, when John Scott died on March 7, just prior to the closing of the session, only John Wallace and Robert Meacham were left among the Negroes in the senate to eulogize his memory.[55] It is impossible to know whether Walls or anyone in his family was ill enough for him to leave Tallahassee. His wife, or his daughter, Nettie, who had been born on November 6, 1878, could have taken ill.[56] Or Walls himself may have suffered a recurrence of his eye or hemorrhoid problems. More likely, however, he just left. Given the political situation, with no clout left to him on any level, it made sense to retire.

52. (Tallahassee) *Weekly Floridian*, January 21, 1879.
53. *Senate Journal, 1879*, p. 162.
54. Ibid., p. 184.
55. Ibid., p. 509.
56. Josiah Walls Pension File.

8

Losing the Battle and the War

A s Florida turned away from Reconstruction and entered the closing decades of the nineteenth century, its political visage was also changing. For the first time since the war, serious Democratic factionalism surfaced, especially after the 1876 election victory of Gov. George F. Drew. Like the Republicans before them, the Democratic party now divided itself over the stakes of office. Many younger Democratic politicians, too young to have participated in the tragic events of the 1860s, were frustrated by the older Democrats' grip on the party machinery and power. This discontent directed against the older, more established, wealthier Civil War veterans was but one element in the factionalism. Many small Florida farmers and businessmen were disgruntled by the seeming lack of concern for their economic position among the state's political leaders. A chief irritant was the state government's policy of speculative land sales to non-Florida developers and railroad builders. This became even more an issue after Gov. William D. Bloxham in 1881 authorized the sale of four million acres of public land to Hamilton Disston, wealthy Philadelphia entrepreneur and land speculator. Although the governor justified the sale as necessary to rescue the huge Internal Improvement Fund debt, "the wave of protest" against it, as well as against the whole system of land dealings by the state government, "formed the keystone" of the independent movement.[1]

The post-Reconstruction period was very difficult for black people in Florida. Their political alternatives were almost nonexistent, as was

1. Edward C. Williamson, "Independentism: A Challenge to the Florida Democracy of 1884."

shown during the 1880s, when Walls with his last few supporters tried to salvage something from the Republican party and from Reconstruction. But the attempt failed. His chief Republican targets were the federal officeholders in East Florida, led primarily by Horatio Bisbee, Jr., congressman in the second district, Dennis Eagan, collector of revenue in Jacksonville, and Malachi Martin, surveyor general in the Gainesville land office.[2] These were men with whom Walls had once joined, but now opposed. In the end, neither tactic worked, and despite the bitterness of the campaigns and desperate measures, Walls was completely and totally defeated; he was unable even to muster sizable black support.

At first, the Negroes were forced to align with the white independents. A black union with the Democrats was impossible; among Negro voters traditional images of slaveholders and slavery were still freshly associated with the Democratic party. It was clear also that while the Democrats encouraged black voting support, Negro leaders could expect to be excluded from positions of power.[3]

There were some concurrent precedents for a black independent position vis-à-vis the major parties outside Florida. As early as 1875 many national black leaders were questioning continued allegiance to the Republican party. P. B. S. Pinchback had arranged a black newspapermen's convention, which met in Cincinnati in August 1875, and there he asked the crucial question: "Can we, by separate action as a people, aid the Republican party to regain its ascendancy in the councils of the nation?"[4] In his 1875 Independence Day oration, Frederick Douglass argued for an independent black movement. Speaking to a large crowd at Hillsdale, Washington, D.C., he warned his listeners: "There are, even in the Republican party, indications of a disposition to get rid of us. Ambitious candidates . . . are already casting about to see if they cannot be elected in some way without the aid of the black vote."[5] By 1883 he was even more outspoken in defending the right of black politicians to seek office in government. In a speech before the national Civil Rights Congress held in Washington that year, Douglass amplified his opinion. "It is no crime to seek or hold office. If it were it would take a larger space than that of Noah's Ark to hold the white criminals. . . . We shall never cease to be a despised and persecuted class while we are known to be excluded by our color from all important positions under

2. Ibid., p. 135.
3. John Wallace to editor, (Tallahassee) *Weekly Floridian*, March 5, 1878.
4. Aptheker, *A Documentary History*, p. 643; *Tallahassee Sentinel*, July 31, 1875.
5. *Tallahassee Sentinel*, July 24, 1875.

the Government."[6] The black New York journalist Timothy Thomas Fortune, whose father Emanuel had been a member of the Conservative bloc in the 1868 Florida constitutional convention, inveighed against the Republican party in 1884 for "having degenerated into an ignoble scramble for place and power. . . . I do not deem it binding upon colored men further to support the Republican party when other more advantageous affiliations can be formed. . . . [However] no colored man can ever claim truthfully to be a Bourbon Democrat. It is a fundamental impossibility. But he can be an independent."[7]

Walls stayed in the background of Florida politics during the first three years of the 1880s. For the most part, it seemed that he had left politics completely. He kept himself occupied, however, for by this time he was widely admired as one of the most successful farmers in the state. One observer who visited his Alachua County plantation in 1883 offered this description of his economic pursuits: "[Walls has] five hundred acres of land under cultivation, lives in one of the finest houses in the county, and employs on his farm the year round from fifty to seventy-five hands. He also owns a sawmill, in the operation of which he gives over twenty-five men constant employment. He also owns about 1,000 acres of land, a good portion of which is divided up into small lots upon which poor colored families are permitted to live, he furnishing them with seed and the necessaries of life until their crops are made when he only requires from them a return of the money advanced and a nominal rental."[8]

An 1883 pamphlet, Charles Henry Webber's *The Eden of the South*, extolled the agricultural virtue of Alachua County. It described Walls then as the largest truck grower in the entire state. According to Webber, Walls himself spent much of his time working in his fields, thereby "taking the lead among his employees."[9] He averaged, for example, 75 crates of tomatoes per acre, and in the particularly good season of 1883, his yield totaled 200 crates per acre. He boxed 6,000 crates that year, and his crop was then sold to a New York shipping firm, Durling and Company. According to Webber, Walls figured his profit on this one crop alone at 47 cents per crate, or $2,280 for the season in tomatoes. His plantation was also described: "Previous to the war, [it] was then considered the best . . . in the State, and upon which was raised more cotton

6. Aptheker, *A Documentary History*, p. 665.
7. Timothy Thomas Fortune, *Black and White: Land, Labor and Politics in the Old South*, p. 132.
8. (Jacksonville) *Florida Times-Union*, September 14, 1884.
9. Pp. 93–94.

per acre than upon any other in the county. It was then upon the border of the great Payne's prairie, which was one of the richest places for cattle-grazing in Florida. Since the prairie became flooded, it has occupied a two-mile frontage on the great Alachua lake, where it has a high bluff and a good beach. The water-front gives excellent transportation facilities by the steamers of the Alachua Navigation Company. These steamers come within a half mile of his house. The plantation is very prettily located between the lake and the Florida Transit Railroad, the nearest shipping station being Arredonda, about two miles distant."[10] It was reputed that he "could get more and better work out of free [Negroes] than any man in the neighborhood."[11] Many Alachua truck farmers, likely including Walls, grew lettuce, cultivating it on large canvas beds, usually 100 × 50 feet, so as to protect the crop from the wind and cold.[12] It is known that Walls invested heavily in orange production. He apparently had one of the larger groves in the county, and when a disastrous freeze occurred in February 1895, he was completely ruined. The year before, however, he reportedly had built a railroad siding onto his property from the main line.[13] Also throughout this period, he had added to his holdings: Ella purchased several acres in her own right in 1882, and three years later, he added another 630 acres for which he paid more than $3,000.[14] Thus, having attained success as a farmer, Walls seemingly had no need to return to the political wars.

The independent movement across the South made its first serious challenge in 1882, and Sen. William Eaton Chandler of New Hampshire assessed its future: "We cannot save the House [of Representatives] without fostering the independent democratic and coalition movements in the southern States. . . . Our straight Republican, carpet-bag, negro

10. The railroad's full title in 1883 was the Florida Transit and Peninsular Railroad; it had merged that year with a small road between Ocala and Waldo. In 1884, it would merge again, this time in consolidation with several smaller roads in the region, forming the Florida Railway and Navigation Company, and in 1888 it would become the northern division of the Florida Central and Peninsular Railway. See Charles Hildreth, "A History of Gainesville, Florida," p. 121.

11. James Henry Roper to E. C. F. Sanchez, n.d., Sanchez Papers.

12. Interview with Miss Etta Means, Gainesville, April 14, 1971. Her father, Lawrence, was a truck farmer specializing in lettuce production on 100 acres north of Gainesville during this period.

13. Interview with Mr. William Jones, Tallahassee, January 14, 1971. Mr. Jones and his father both worked for Josiah Walls on the agricultural farm of present-day Florida A & M University during the early twentieth century. Mr. Jones, now in his late eighties, stated that Walls often was given to reminiscing about his Gainesville farm.

14. Deed Book O, p. 810, Deed Book W, p. 69, Clerk of the Circuit Court, Alachua County Courthouse.

governments, whether fairly or unfairly, have been destroyed and cannot be revived."[15]

In the second congressional district in East Florida, Horatio Bisbee and Jesse J. Finley were again the candidates for the House of Representatives. Neither Leonard Dennis nor Walls, still united, were campaigning for the Republican Bisbee. According to Republican former comptroller Clayton Cowgill, Dennis was only "lukewarm" and Walls "secretly antagonistic" about Bisbee.[16] Both were even more opposed than Cowgill assumed. On August 11, 1882, at Roper's Hall in Gainesville, the Walls-Dennis faction clashed with Bisbee's supporters in the local convention to select delegates to the district meeting scheduled for Jacksonville two weeks later. (Prior to that meeting, Walls and Dennis had clashed for a brief period, but their dispute again was healed, this time by early July.)[17]

United with Dennis, Walls declared he would attend the Jacksonville convention not only as an Alachua delegate, but also as a candidate for Congress. This announcement "brought down the house" in Roper's Hall. Several resolutions were passed denouncing Bisbee, and the Alachua County delegation was instructed to vote as a unit for Walls.[18] The Gainesville *Weekly Bee* did not believe that he was intent on making a serious bid but rather was more interested in harassing Bisbee. The paper commented that Walls would swing back to the regulars "at the proper time," as he and Bisbee were "pards."[19] The *Bee*'s assessment was based upon its own analysis of the independent movement, which "in the South would mean nothing without the affiliation of the colored man. But even with his assistance such a movement can not attain to a thoroughly organized party. If the Northern Republicans—the officeholders—are excluded, the full strength of the colored vote will not be polled . . . while if [they] are admitted, former Democrats will not affiliate with them."[20]

Walls sent his delegation to Jacksonville, having fully considered the import of his own independent campaign. At the meeting his supporters sent up a trial balloon by placing his name in nomination. When no further support materialized, Dennis immediately withdrew the nomination, and in support of Walls the entire Alachua delegation withdrew

15. Chandler to James G. Blaine, October 2, 1882, Chandler Papers, vol. 56.
16. Clayton Cowgill to Chandler, October 24, 1882, ibid.
17. See (Gainesville) *Weekly Bee*, June 9, July 7, 21, 1882.
18. Ibid., August 18, 1882.
19. Ibid., August 11, 1882.
20. Ibid., May 19, 1882.

from the convention. Bisbee won renomination unanimously and went on to win a close election from Finley. Walls and Dennis did not oppose Bisbee further, but their actions seemed a test for the campaign two years hence.

Following the election, J. Willis Menard prophesied those events which would force Negroes into an independent race. In a letter to Chandler, a member of the national Republican executive committee, he warned: "If the Administration desires to carry this state in 1884, it will have to make certain changes, and place men in Federal positions who will work in harmony with the leading colored men in the State, and thereby present a united front to the Bourbon enemy in the next struggle. All the leading colored men in the State favored the Independent movement."[21]

Walls went after Bisbee seriously in 1884. As early as February it became clear that he intended to battle Bisbee for the Republican nomination to Congress and, if necessary, to carry the battle outside the party by an independent campaign. He was aided by the fact that the Democrats who were disaffected with their party elders had also developed full-blown into an independent organization. The white independents launched their campaign for the state government by nominating Frank Pope and Jonathan Greeley as candidates for governor and lieutenant governor, respectively, at their Live Oak conference on June 18. Pope was a Madison County lawyer and state senator who had been a long-time member of the Democratic party. Jacksonville businessman Greeley, on the other hand, had been an original Florida Republican. He was a co-organizer with Ossian B. Hart of the Union-Republican Club of Jacksonville, which had sponsored the first state Republican convention in Reconstruction. In 1884 Jonathan Greeley was also in the state senate.[22]

The Live Oak platform reflected in large measure the independents' disgust with corruption in Florida politics and government. Both Democrats and Republicans came under fire. Both parties were no longer "guided by the principles that gave them existence and are utterly lacking in all the elements which invite intelligent, patriotic support. Run in party grooves for party ends, they antagonize the public welfare and sacrifice the dearest rights of the people to the moloch of race

21. J. Willis Menard to Chandler, November 27, 1882, Chandler Papers, vol. 57.
22. See biographical sketches of the candidates, in "Independent Platform and Record of the Candidates," Charles Lewis Papers.

prejudice, that party hate may be kept burning and the insatiate greed of the office-holder appeased."[23]

The Democrats were specifically accused of several abuses since 1876: failure to reform "the present autocratic constitution"; wasteful policies involving public land sales (especially the Disston purchase and the nullification of the law which enabled small Florida settlers to buy land at twenty-five cents per acre); association with corporate interests opposed to the people's will; their method of paying "for party service out of the pockets of the people"; their "lavish" land grants to Florida railroads; their fostering of "party hate and racial antagonisms"; and their political opposition to a free press and the independent movement that would prevent party leaders from going "unrebuked of their wrongs."[24]

To correct these abuses and institute reform, the Live Oak delegates adopted a wide range of goals on which to build their campaign. They advocated "a free ballot, a full vote, and a fair count"; they called for a constitutional convention, a free press, a railroad commission, a local option law to legislate temperance, "free and unrestricted suffrage without educational or property qualifications," a reform of the existing election code, an end of land sales to speculators, economy in government spending, and support for immigration to Florida.[25] It was the type of platform designed to appeal to the most diverse groups among the electorate.

It appealed to Josiah Walls. Yet, even before he and Bisbee faced off in East Florida's 1884 congressional campaign, independents were already preparing to fight the latter's nomination. "Anti-ring" letters warned of an independent candidate who would oppose Bisbee if he decided to run again: "Take notice, that if it is discovered that . . . the officeholders are travelling in the different counties for the purpose of packing delegates . . . a convention will be called immediately from the people and a nomination made. Don't let the 'Machine' rest on the people too heavy." Among the various names besides Walls' mentioned as alternatives to Bisbee were Joseph Lee, a black lawyer from Jacksonville, Jonathan C. Greeley, who had already accepted the independent nomination as lieutenant governor, and Dennis.[26]

A state conference of Negroes was convened in Gainesville on February 5, 1884. It was organized chiefly at the urging of J. Willis Menard,

23. Ibid.
24. Ibid.
25. Ibid.
26. (Jacksonville) *The Florida Journal*, May 29, 1884.

and had been called to consider the future role for blacks in Florida's political process. More than 200 delegates attended as the meeting opened in Roper's Hall at 11:00 A.M. Menard was chosen chairman; in his opening address he underscored the need for Florida's black people to reconsider their loyalties to the Republican party. He recalled that his race had stood with the party since the war, but there now was "an emergency which the colored had to contend with." It was his view that it was no longer feasible to maintain Republican strength in the state and, as a result, the Negroes "were now ready to affiliate with any liberal party who [sic] would give them recognition."[27] This meeting disturbed several prominent white Republicans who were uneasy about the potential of a black independent movement. It was suggested that some white Republicans should attend the Gainesville convention and exert whatever pacifying influence they could, as "those who will constitute the personnel of this conference will represent the bulk of the Republican organization" in Florida.[28]

Among other business conducted at the meeting, two delegates were chosen to attend the National Colored Convention, and education, temperance, mechanic arts, and civil rights discussions also took place. The conference adopted a platform which outlined its goals in the coming elections:

(1) We want increased facilities of common school education and the higher branches, so as to be able to reduce the high rate of illiteracy which the last census shows to exist among our people in this State.

(2) We want a fair representation on juries, and a fair show in the courts and before justices of the peace.

(3) We want to cast our votes freely and have them fairly counted; and also a better system of voter registration.

(4) We want a fair recognition and representation in the offices of the State and county, and also under city government.

(5) We want to enjoy the same rights and privileges accorded to others in public places, on railroads and steamers, when we pay the same fare.

(6) We want a law enacted restoring to the right of suffrage all men (most of whom are colored) disfranchised for alleged petty offenses tried before justices of the peace.[29]

27. *Fernandina Mirror*, February 9, 1884; (Jacksonville) *Florida Times-Union*, February 6, 1884.

28. James Dean to Chandler, January 14, 1884, Chandler Papers, vol. 59.

29. *Fernandina Mirror*, February 9, 1884.

The convention also established an executive committee, to which Walls was elected, empowered to determine the best policy and party to carry out these aims.

The results of the conference were clear: Florida's black leaders had decided upon an independent political course. This at least was the conclusion of R. W. Rute, a Florida Republican, when he read the account of the meeting. In a letter to a friend he observed that as a result of the meeting, the Negroes were "to a man in favor of cutting loose from the federal officeholders as a class, and will refuse to be led by them any longer. . . . Our intelligent colored men have no confidence in these would-be white leaders. . . . The Resolutions of the . . . convention were almost unanimous in favor of joining the Independents, entirely unanimous."[30]

In June 1884, the national Republican party gathered in Chicago to nominate a candidate to succeed Chester Arthur as president. In the same auditorium where James Garfield was chosen four years before, James G. Blaine outlasted Arthur for the nomination.[31]

Although not a member of the Florida delegation, Walls was considered for a seat on the national Republican committee. His possible appointment reflected the split and internal disputes within the organization in Florida. The regulars or officeholders were opposed to Walls, while Joseph Lee, an advocate of reform and "anti-ring," supported his nomination. The first choice proposed was Edward Cheney, but the committee was unable to agree upon him. The second choice was Maj. Joseph Durkee of Jacksonville, but he was declared ineligible as an existing federal appointee. The committee then centered on Walls. John A. Long, member of the Florida Republican delegation, upon his return from Chicago, affirmed that Walls indeed had been seriously considered but that Lee had remained adamantly opposed to his selection. Long explained that after the failure to place Cheney and Durkee on the national committee he agreed to support Walls on the urging of Dennis Eagan. When Lee, however, refused to change his vote on the matter, J. D. Cole, a Republican from St. Augustine, was elected instead. According to Long, Joseph Lee could have placed Walls on the national committee with relative ease as the chairman of the Florida delegation. He added in his own defense that there were two reasons why he had not originally sponsored Walls. First, Walls had not indicated his wish to

30. R. W. Rute to [?] Crandall, February 27, 1884, Sanford Papers.
31. *New York Times*, June 1–6, 1884.

become a member of the Republican national committee, and second, against the opposition of Lee he had no chance to win the seat.[32]

Lee, of course, protested vehemently that Long's version of the affair in Chicago was false. According to him, it had been the opposition of the regulars led by Eagan and Long that had kept Walls from winning. Lee added that this was but another reason why there needed to be an independent campaign.[33] Walls himself made no recorded comment about his treatment at the Chicago convention; however, it is likely to have confirmed his intent to oppose Bisbee and his faction in the congressional race.

Walls began his own efforts to wrest the Republican nomination at the Alachua County convention held in Roper's Hall on June 28, 1884. He issued the call as county executive chairman, and its purpose was to select two slates of delegates, one to attend the July 29 state convention in Tallahassee which would nominate Republican candidates for governor and lieutenant governor, and the other to go to the district nominating convention in Fernandina on July 9, where the Republican candidate for Congress from the second electoral district would be chosen. Walls' position was clear; he had demanded an independent convention, not a Republican meeting. Alachua County Republicans rallied behind him and an independent campaign. The Fernandina-bound delegates were instructed to vote as a unit for Walls, and the reporter who covered the proceedings noted no negative votes and only one voice opposed to the resolution. Walls headed the group going to Tallahassee, and Dennis was chairman of the Fernandina delegation. He and Walls attended both meetings, however.[34]

At Fernandina, Dennis, as head of the eleven-man county contingent, placed Walls' name in nomination against incumbent Horatio Bisbee. But from the beginning it seemed as if the meeting was stacked against the Alachua rebels. The chairman was Greeley, who hoped to unite East Florida regulars and independents behind Bisbee. Greeley denied Dennis' motion to exclude several of the county delegations. "The Little Giant" contended that many had been in violation of the rules for nominating conventions established by the state central committee. There was supposed to be a five-day hiatus between local and district or state conventions. Few of the other delegations, Dennis argued, had met this requirement; thus they were ineligible to vote. Greeley disagreed,

32. (Jacksonville) *The Florida Journal*, June 16, 19, 1884.
33. Ibid., June 19, 1884.
34. Ibid., July 3, 1884.

however, and he rejected the motion after the Alachua delegates "had made a great deal of noise and displayed a great deal of irritation." The bid went to Bisbee by a 71 to 12 margin. Walls added but one vote from an unknown Suwannee County man to his unit vote from Alachua. The dissidents walked out upon hearing the final results, and at another meeting, also in Fernandina that day, Walls embarked on his own independent campaign.[35]

A rally was held three days later in Gainesville. Ella was severely ill at the time, so Walls did not address the crowd. Many blacks and a sprinkling of whites turned out and the tension between the factions was evident, although they did not divide only on racial lines. During the rally, held outdoors in downtown Gainesville near the courthouse square, F. D. Hughes, a Walls supporter and the local white candidate for the state senate, was shot and wounded slightly by Caesar Joiner, an off-duty black city policeman. Joiner was an ardent Bisbee follower. Although he claimed Hughes had fired first, he was arrested; subsequently, he was released.[36]

Because of the confusion caused by this and other incidents during the day, newspaper accounts conflicted as to whether Walls actually had been endorsed by county Republicans. According to one paper, he was "out" as a candidate as a result of the rally, while another man who was there insisted he had been "fully ratified" by a majority of those present.[37]

The political scene in East Florida was further complicated by the differing views among many leading Republicans on an independent ticket of any kind. *The Florida Journal* editorialized, by way of illustration, that there were as many opinions of the proper Republican approach as there were Republicans to offer them: "Bisbee supports the Independent State ticket [Pope and Greeley] and is the regular nominee for Congress. Dennis opposes the Independent State ticket and supports the Independent candidate for Congress [Walls]. [Edward] Cheney opposes all 'Independents' and goes for straightout Republican nominations or nothing. [Dennis] Eagan favors an 'Independent' State ticket, but opposes Pope. So, you see, things are a little mixed."[38]

35. Ibid., July 10, 1884.
36. Ibid., July 17, 1884; this or another similar incident at the rally may have provoked the comment that in Gainesville after the rally, "there is a heap of talking and fussing," described in a letter to Charles, July 14, 1884, James B. Bailey Papers, Southern Historical Collection.
37. (Jacksonville) *The Florida Journal*, July 17, 1884; *Fernandina Mirror*, July 19, 1884.
38. July 14, 1884.

Despite the complications, certain aspects of the situation stood out. First, much of the Walls-Bisbee feud rested on mutual personal dislike. At best Bisbee had been only a tepid supporter of Walls when he was running for Congress. Moreover, there probably was a natural jealousy between the man supplanted and the man who succeeded him in a position of prestige and power. Second, the two men conflicted in principle over the need for reform within the Republican party. Bisbee's position was clear; besides being a federal officeholder himself, he had backed James G. Blaine at the national convention in Chicago rather than Chester Arthur, the reformers' candidate. Walls, on the other hand, had long since realized that the Republican party had failed to keep its commitment to equality. His people had received little from the years of Republican control, and most of that lay in jeopardy in 1884. Third, the two men were in close competition for the same votes. For much of the period after 1870, Walls had commanded and gained overwhelming obedience from East Florida Negroes who voted in the elections, but following his eclipse as a national figure and the steady disfranchisement of black voters through the courts and other forms of institutional intimidation, those votes had become open to outside, non-Negro influence. Moreover, there were fewer Republicans proportionally in the state by 1884. The steady stream of white immigration had brought with it more and more Democrats. Both Walls and Bisbee realized that they were struggling for fewer votes at a time when more were needed to overcome the opposition. These considerations led to an especially bitter campaign, besmirched by emotional name-calling and crude campaign tactics on both sides. Nor did either candidate pay much attention to the Democratic candidate, Charles Dougherty.[39]

A few weeks following the Fernandina meeting, the state Republican gubernatorial convention met in Tallahassee at Gallie's Hall on July 27. Both Walls and Dennis attended. From the outset it was clear that the independent wing of the party was in command, thereby assuring Pope and Greeley positions as its standard-bearers. It fell to a Putnam County delegate named Hines to offer a resolution that pledged the Republican party to Pope and Greeley with "undivided support." Unfortunately the resolution could not hide the greatly divided sentiments in the convention. Dennis, for example, while supporting Walls for Congress, remained adamantly opposed to a state independent ticket. He vehemently denounced the Hines resolution. His outburst in turn evoked a heated

39. The beginning of Dougherty's campaign is described in a letter, L. D. Huston to Maria Huston, August 6, 1884, L. D. Huston Papers.

response from the independents in the hall, and a lengthy and emotional debate ensued. It was finally brought to a halt by Walls, whose observations were sufficient to still the argument. He stated that he too did not favor the resolution, as it required the Republican party to nominate Pope and Greeley. However, his reasons were far more political than personal. "The Republicans of my county sent a delegation to Live Oak to nominate Pope and Greeley, and we are here today instructed to endorse that nomination. They are now the candidates of the Independent party, as such we can elect them; but the moment we nominate them by call of counties, they become our candidates, and you give the Democrats a club to break their heads."[40] His logic worked: the independents were endorsed, but were not nominated by the Republican convention.

The East Florida race opened in earnest in mid-August. From his congressional offices in Washington, Bisbee challenged Walls to debate his record in several mutual campaign stops. Walls replied by open letter on August 14:

> Your letter . . . challenging me or any person that I may select to meet you at your meetings during your canvass, is highly characteristic of you.
>
> The methods that you use to perpetuate your official arrogance have driven from you a large majority of your former friends, and the manner in which you have ignored my people who have heretofore formed a large majority of your supporters, are among the many reasons why you should not be elected to the Forty Ninth Congress.
>
> The assertion that I have repeatedly declared that I had no hope of an election but simply lead a bolt to defeat you is false, *in toto*, and is used by you . . . to divert attention from your political methods, by which you obtained your so-called nomination. . . .
>
> I accept your challenge, and will meet you in person or otherwise, as proposed by you, and will show more than one reason why you should not be supported by all or any of the Republicans of this District.[41]

In closing he added that he wanted to debate, on the "broad plane" of independentism, the issue of party reforms as outlined at the Live Oak and Gainesville conferences. Bisbee responded curtly, informing him

40. (Tallahassee) *Land of Flowers*, July 29, 1884.
41. (Jacksonville) *The Florida Journal*, August 21, 1884.

that under no circumstances would their debate move beyond Bisbee's own congressional record.

Even before Bisbee returned to Florida to begin his campaign, Walls and Mathew M. Lewey began publishing a newspaper in Gainesville, *The Farmer's Journal.* The first issue asserted the paper's emphasis upon agricultural topics of interest to Alachua County farmers; however, that same issue also carried a lengthy article, appearing under Walls' name, attacking Horatio Bisbee. The paper was meant as a forum for Walls; unfortunately, there are no known copies preserved. He used his first chance to charge his Republican opponent with having exerted "undue influence and corrupt tactics" to win the nomination at Fernandina. These tactics supposedly included promises of offices in exchange for votes and payment of expenses incurred by the delegates at the convention. Walls defended his right to contest the Republican nominee despite the outcome of the party meeting on the grounds that since he had not chosen to run as a Republican, he was "not bound to support the 'self nominated' candidate." The article concluded with advice to the black voter to "show . . . that we can act upon political matters without fear; that we will not vote for or endorse the nominees of corrupt and lying ringsters and politicians simply because they have . . . secured the declaration that they are the regular nominees."[42]

Bisbee formally opened his reelection campaign on September 1, before a largely partisan crowd in St. James Park (present-day Hemming Park) in Jacksonville. Although this was the first opportunity for the two men to debate in person, Ella was still ill and Walls would not leave her alone; the "Little Giant," accompanied by F. E. Hughes and Lewey, traveled to Jacksonville instead. Dennis claimed that under the terms of the challenge he had the right to share the speakers' stand for the debate. Bisbee refused, and the band which had been hired by the congressman drowned out Dennis when he tried to address the crowd of some 300. It was reported that Dennis left the park in disgust and continued downtown. Before leaving, however, he warned of things to come in the campaign. In an interview with a Jacksonville reporter Dennis intimated that Bisbee could expect similar treatment when he came to Gainesville. "Bisbee is on his own ground here, and is boss; but he'll be up in Alachua at the end of the week, and if we don't give him a picnic then you may set Dennis down for a flunk."[43]

42. (Jacksonville) *Florida Times-Union*, September 4, 1884; (Jacksonville) *The Florida Journal*, August 28, 1884.

43. (Jacksonville) *Florida Times-Union*, September 2, 1884.

On September 6, Bisbee arrived in Gainesville for a rally in Oak Hall Grove, just southeast of the courthouse. The events that occurred that day were classified as "rich, rare and racy."[44] Coming north from a rally the day before in Ocala, some forty miles away, Bisbee stepped from the train at noon. There he was met by a Dr. Ambrose, chairman of the Gainesville rally, and a Negro marching band hired for the occasion. As the rally was not to begin until later, a procession escorted Bisbee through Gainesville's streets and out to the grove. Once there, Bisbee, his advisors, his hosts, and the band waited for the crowds to assemble. By 1:00 P.M. there were approximately 1,000 people gathered in front of the platform that had been erected.

Bisbee began his address, during the middle of which Walls and F. D. Hughes arrived on the scene. Walls took a seat on the end of the stand and sat quietly for about twenty minutes, apparently listening to his opponent's speech. He then leaned over to Charles Webber, reporter and author of *Eden of the South* who was covering the rally, and asked him in a whisper: "Do you think Bisbee would allow me to interrupt him for a moment?" When Webber did not reply, Walls arose, "fumbling in his pocket for some papers," and interrupted the proceedings. The onlookers in the crowd, who had remained up to this moment fairly quiet, roared their approval of Walls' efforts to take over from Bisbee. The latter waved Walls back to his seat and asked for silence so as to continue his speech. Neither Walls nor the crowd was in a mood to grant his requests. Walls asked whether or not he was going to have the right to debate his opponent, according to the terms of the challenge.

"By and by," replied Bisbee.

"Will you do it, will you do it, will you do it," Walls screamed in rapid sequence, "for, by God, I demand it."

After this exchange Walls did sit back down and Bisbee went on, explaining the complexities of free trade, protectionism, and the issue of federal appointments. He claimed that many Negroes had been appointed to federal offices in Florida; however, he warned that no more would be appointed from Alachua County until this factionalism had ceased and he was given his due as the regular nominee of the Republican party. He closed his speech with an allusion to the now famous challenge to Walls. He would allow his opponent twenty or thirty minutes to address the crowd, but first, Mr. Pierson of his campaign committee would speak. Accordingly Dr. Ambrose, the chairman, stood up to

44. The information in the following paragraphs relating to the Gainesville rally is from the *Florida Times-Union*, September 10, 1884.

introduce the next speaker. Walls took the rostrum before Ambrose could finish his task. Wheeling around to confront his adversary amidst a "stupendous uproar," he again asked for his rights, punctuating his demand with "By God, I'll have my rights or I'll die right here."

Bisbee surrendered. He retired to the far end of the platform and lit a cigar while the pro-Walls crowd continued to chant their leader's name over and over. Confusion reigned as several Bisbee supporters protested. Police moved in to arrest the more disruptive persons as the band played, the crowd chanted, and Walls made an unsuccessful plea to be heard. When the pandemonium at last subsided, he began his emotional attack on Bisbee: "Colonel Bisbee says *The Farmer's Journal* published by me and paid for by me, is paid for by Democratic money. When he says this he lies. I say he lies! I say he lies!! I say he *lies*!!! . . . Intelligent people—you people before me—we know what he wants; he wants only to elect himself. He can go to hell. He cannot know whether a Democrat ever paid me a cent. I am able to fight him, and I mean to fight him to the death. We will kill him. We will fight him till the election night. . . . He has lied to me, and he has lied about me, and he talks to me, and he talks to you, as if we are fools. I know about these things. What are your interests? Are they not identical with the interests of the people among whom you live? Let Bisbee go to hell." By this time the noise of the crowd was so great that he could only add: "Let me tell you another thing. . . ." Then he gave way to Dennis. The "Little Giant" took care to record fully his treatment in Jacksonville at Bisbee's hands. He closed by asking the crowd to consider the qualities of Josiah Walls: "We offer a man who belongs with you, who is one of you; your ways are his ways, and his ways are your ways; he has invested his property here; he has been to Congress and represented you there with honor to himself and you. Nothing can be said against the honor and integrity of J. T. Walls." Dennis had plenty to say about the honor and integrity of Horatio Bisbee, however. "You can not trust [him]. He said he was coming down here to clean us out. Has he done it? Are we going to let him do it?" The overwhelming rush of cheers gave out the answer. Then, Hughes took his turn to urge support for Walls. At last Pierson was allowed to speak.

In a few minutes, Walls again was on his feet to interrupt, and the same reaction was recorded from the onlookers. Charles H. Webber described Walls at that precise moment, standing on the speaker's platform with arms outstretched and raised "as a minister . . . about to pronounce a benediction." There he stood and received the swelling approval of those in attendance. Once the noise had abated his words could again be heard: "Today we have listened quietly to what Bisbee had to say; we did not prevent his full and free utterances. . . . I am fighting Bisbee to the bitter end. I have money of my own. If he challenges me and changes the code, I am the man to meet him on any point. . . . We must crush them or die. . . . Will you stand by me?" Once more his supporters in the audience cheered their approbation. There were a few more remarks in conclusion, and then the rally adjourned. Bisbee had been given his Alachua County picnic.

Nine days after the meeting Walls granted an interview with Charles Webber in which the two men discussed what had happened at Oak Hall Grove. The interview took place in the office of *The Farmer's Journal* on September 15, as Walls and Lewey were preparing another edition publishing the rest of his campaign schedule. When asked if he were sorry for having said the things he did, Walls replied: "Oh no; under the circumstances I would say them again." Walls confessed that he was angry when he went to the meeting place. He had been informed that he would not be admitted or allowed to speak, and it had seemed to him that Bisbee was intent on repeating his Jacksonville act. Moreover, he admitted to "not being myself," having had, perhaps, too much to drink before the rally, but he distinguished between stimulation and intoxication, asserting that he was not drunk at all. He was further disturbed by the fact that he was, in his own opinion, probably overtired from having nursed his sick wife for three weeks. Walls explained his queer behavior as a result of these conditions. "When angered I always stammer and stutter, and my ideas come so fast they interfere with clear expressions. I was not drunk, but I was mentally and physically weak." Furthermore, he had a cold, and claimed he went to the rally intending not to speak at all, but rather to insure that Bisbee would allow one of his supporters, Hughes or Dennis for example, to address the audience according to the challenge. That brought up the matter of the papers he carried in his pocket. Walls said it was a copy of the invitation to debate Bisbee. He did admit that his faction meant quite deliberately to disrupt the rally in the hope of ending Bisbee's own "abusiveness." He himself had achieved a large measure of personal satisfaction in meting out insults to Bisbee in return. But it had been also a necessary thing to do. "We had to do it, or forever hold our peace." At the end of the interview, Walls once again confirmed his intention to stay in the race and insisted that his money was his own, that he was no "tool of the Democrats," and that Bisbee would always be "an enemy to our race in disguise."[45]

45. Ibid., September 17, 1884.

Despite his wife's illness, Walls carried on an active campaign. His stops from the middle of September to the November 4 election included more than thirty separate speeches in as many different locales in East Florida. In Jacksonville on September 18, before a crowd estimated at more than 500, he expressed his preference for Dougherty over Bisbee.[46] The bitterness of the feud distressed many. In a letter to Henry S. Sanford in September 1884, S. H. Adams observed: "Gen. Walls and Bisbee are fighting hard and had we funds, could defeat Bisbee. No money from the National Committee and Bisbee has managed to kill off most of our Republican friends in Jacksonville who were disposed to help us."[47]

As the candidate who could best insure a Democratic victory by splitting Republican votes, Walls received sympathetic, if cynical, coverage in East Florida's major Democratic newspapers. The *Fernandina Mirror*, for example, editorialized: "We admire the plain, straightforward firmness of Mr. Walls's acceptance of Mr. Bisbee's challenge. He speaks as a man conscious of his own firmness of position, as one not to be bluffed or put down."[48] And when a Democrat wrote to ask *The Florida Journal* why he was referred to as "General Walls" when "there appears on record no indication that [he] did anything or learned anything in Congress except to sign the payroll 'his x mark,' " the paper replied that had the writer lived in the state for a decent length of time, he would have known of Walls' qualifications and would hardly have needed to write such a letter.[49]

By mid-October Bisbee was at least scared, although he had little reason to be, according to the election results. On Tuesday, October 14, Walls arrived in Fernandina for an evening rally in the Lyceum Hall. He had come to defend himself against the old charges that he was in the race only to split votes, and he also wanted to answer an accusation that some of his supporters had made Democratic speeches there earlier. As he made his way to the lecture hall with Dennis and Hughes from the train station, a Bisbee supporter intercepted him. According to the published reports, Walls then and there was offered a bribe. If he would pull out of the congressional race, any federal appointment in East Florida was his for the asking. Walls refused, and when he entered the hall, he discovered a band which had been hired by Bisbee to break up

46. Ibid., September 13, 19, October 5, 8, 9, 11, 1884.
47. S. H. Adams to Sanford, September 16, 1884, Sanford Papers.
48. *Fernandina Mirror*, August 30, 1884.
49. August 21, 1884.

the rally and lead the audience to a Bisbee gathering nearby. Walls was unable to deliver his address.[50]

It was also reported at this time that Bisbee returned to Washington to complain about Walls to the national Republican committee. He apparently wanted that organization "to interfere in his behalf and persuade or compel Walls to come down." Walls, however, still maintained his intention to stay in the campaign, and Mathew Lewey predicted he would win, polling more than 1,000 votes in Alachua County alone.[51]

While the two Republicans were at each other's throats, Charles Dougherty, the Democratic nominee, was waging a smooth campaign. Wherever he went in East Florida there were large and enthusiastic crowds. He could attack Bisbee's record without much fear of reprisal. Clearly it was true, as one paper suggested, that while "Bisbee and Walls are having their fun . . . Dougherty scoops in the votes."[52]

The results of the election sharpened the irony of the entire campaign. Nowhere was there a significant measure of support for Walls, and the early returns from Gainesville indicated that even in his stronghold his total was light. It was not even enough to help defeat Bisbee. Charles Dougherty had managed that by himself, polling 16,895 votes to Bisbee's 15,595. Walls' total in the second electoral district was only 215 votes.[53] Thus the bitterness, the expenditures, and the time invested were all a waste for Josiah Walls. Simply and completely, his political career had ended.

50. *Fernandina Mirror*, October 18, 1884.
51. (Jacksonville) *Florida Times-Union*, October 5, 9, 1884.
52. (Tallahassee) *Land of Flowers*, September 20, 1884.
53. (Tallahassee) *Weekly Floridian*, November 11, 1884. Walls polled only 149 votes in Alachua County. These were his largest totals in the district. Bisbee, on the other hand, polled almost 2,000 votes in Alachua County alone. See ibid., December 9, 1884.

9

Epilogue

D URING the last twenty years of his life, Walls encountered personal tragedy, financial misfortune, and the afflictions of old age. No doubt the impact of the first two hastened the coming of the latter. On New Year's Day 1885, Ella Fergueson Walls died, leaving her husband a widower after nineteen years of marriage, with Nettie, their six-year-old child. Walls married Ella Angeline Gass, his first wife's cousin, on July 5, 1885. She was not very much older than Nettie, being but fourteen when she and Walls recited their vows before the Reverend Peter McRae in Gainesville.[1] Those who remember them describe their relationship as distant and formal; he seemed much closer to Nettie.[2]

There is almost no information available about this period in his life. Yet, he did make one last try at least for a seat in the state legislature. On September 29, 1890, at Simpson's opera house in Gainesville, the Alachua County Republicans met in convention. Walls was still the executive chairman. He was nominated for the state senate, and William Cessna for the state assembly, by acclamation. It was hardly a contest, and the best Walls could hope for was support in the western half of the county. "Gen. Walls has given up the contest as far as the eastern part of the county is concerned. In spite of his efforts, the colored voters are openly supporting the regular nominees of the democratic party against

1. Josiah Walls Pension File. She was the widow of Walls and remarried one year after his death; as Ella A. Walls Smith, she unsuccessfully filed for a pension in 1907. Her records are in the National Archives in Walls' file, and there is no cross-reference.
2. This was the opinion of two people who observed them together on many occasions: interviews with Mrs. E. R. Jones, Tallahassee, January 15, 1971, and with William Jones, January 16, 1971. (They are not related.)

independent democrats nominated by the wire-pulling republicans." Of course, Walls could not "pull wires" in the fashion of Reconstruction days, and the old independent campaigner had little chance to win. The final results showed that J. A. Rosborough scored an overwhelming victory, but Walls did carry Arredondo and Archer.[3]

Shortly thereafter, he was again struck down by the physical ailments that had plagued him since the Civil War. He filed for and received a $12 per month pension in 1891. According to a neighbor, Walls at this time was "unable to do anything like an able-bodied man's work, in fact he can do about 1/3 as much. . . . The symptoms . . . are of the most serious and violent nature. He is unable to breathe clearly, and has the most excruciating pains."[4] A. J. Parker, who had also attended the first Mrs. Walls, testified that he was suffering from "chronic disease of the stomach and eyes, occasioned by degenerated liver."[5]

To add to his problems, the severe freeze of February 1895 ruined him financially. He apparently had invested heavily in oranges, and the freeze destroyed his groves and vegetable crops. In poor health and ruined materially, Walls moved his family to Tallahassee where he became the director of the farm at Florida Normal College (now Florida A & M University), possibly at the urging of William Sheats, state superintendent of public instruction.[6] He replaced W. A. Cuppage, who, it seems, was more interested in veterinary medicine than in agriculture. On the other hand, Walls continually worried about the college and the farm, the lack of money, and the inadequate equipment. He spent most of his time in the fields that lay below the Tallahassee hills on which the college was built. He never wore farm clothes or coveralls, but rather preferred to dress in "working suits," the attire of a large and successful man. However, soon after he arrived he instituted techniques of farming new to the college: most important were terrace farming and a new way of plowing to prevent soil erosion, a common problem in Cuppage's term.[7]

While in the fields Walls would sometimes talk of his farming days in Gainesville, but he never mentioned his past political career. Nor did he become involved in local Tallahassee affairs, either politically or socially. He was looked upon as "a race-pride man"; as such, he was thought too

3. *Gainesville Sun*, September 30, October 16, November 6, 1890.
4. Josiah Walls Pension File, affidavit of A. L. Pierce, January 19, 1891.
5. Ibid., affidavit of A. J. Parker.
6. Interview with William Jones.
7. Leedell Neyland and John W. Riley, *The History of Florida Agricultural and Mechanical University*, p. 24; interview with William Jones.

black for the white community and too intelligent for the black. As a result he spent his leisure time at home, primarily reading.[8] Home for the Wallses was a little white frame house he purchased from J. F. Montgomery in 1900 for $350.[9]

Sometime during this period (about 1900, but the exact date is unknown) tragedy again struck Josiah Walls. His daughter Nettie, who had been thought of as a "quiet girl," "very handsome," "intelligent and friendly," and "fond of children," apparently underwent a radical change in behavior. No longer did she care to play with the children in the neighborhood, combing their hair and singing to them as she had been fond of doing. Instead she became a recluse of sorts, shutting herself in the house for long periods of time, venturing out only to chase away curious visitors or else to shoot at the birds and squirrels in the yard. Then, on a bright and sunny day sometime around the turn of the century, Nettie killed a little girl, Maggie Gibbs. According to Mrs. E. R. Jones, an elderly Tallahassee woman who had been one of Nettie's "children," on that particular day Walls had gotten up early and headed down the hill to the blacksmith's shop with a scythe which needed fixing slung over his shoulder. On his way he passed Mrs. Jones, then a young girl "not yet ten," who was outside playing in her own yard. Soon after he disappeared, and after Ella had gone to her job teaching school, a shot rang out from the Walls home. Nettie rushed out, passed by the bewildered Mrs. Jones and others who quickly gathered at the sound, and ran down the hill. Inside it was discovered that Maggie Gibbs, daughter of a minister, had been stabbed and shot in one of the closets. A short while later, Walls and Nettie came home. He was in a state of shock, apparently refusing to believe that such a thing had happened.

One aspect of the murder was revenge; Nettie had been seeing Maggie's father, a widower, for some time. However, they had broken up their relationship shortly before the murder. In any event, based upon her peculiar behavior, she was sent to the state mental institution at Chattahoochee, where she died "six weeks, or six months," after her arrival.[10] Her death took its toll on Walls, who never recovered.

His own death came on May 15, 1905, around noon.[11] He was buried in a Negro cemetery in Tallahassee, most likely after a small funeral

---

8. Interview with William Jones.
9. Deed Book LL, Clerk of the Circuit Court, Leon County Courthouse, Tallahassee.
10. Interview with Mrs. E. R. Jones.
11. Josiah Walls Pension File, Ella A. Walls Smith records. Note that this date does not agree with the *Biographical Directory of the American Congress, 1774–1961*, p. 1769.

service attended by close friends and his widow. There are no published accounts of his death, no will probated, and no death certificate filed with the state of Florida.[12] Thus, in much the same way as he was born and spent his life, Josiah Walls died—surrounded by incomplete details and gaps in the historical record.

12. The death certificate, if one were available, would be in the Bureau of Vital Statistics, Jacksonville, and a will, if one were probated, would be in the probate records in the Leon County Courthouse. The absence of both, combined with the more news-worthy death of Confederate General Fitzhugh Lee that same week, accounts for the complete reliance on the widow's records in the National Archives. There were several Negro cemeteries in Tallahassee in 1905; however, many have since been destroyed.

Bibliography of Works Cited

PRIMARY SOURCES

American Annual Cyclopaedia and Register of Important Events of the Year 1867. New York: D. Appleton and Company, 1868.

American Missionary Archives. Correspondence and Reports, Amistad Research Center, Dillard University, New Orleans. Microfilm copy, University of Florida.

Bailey, James B. Papers. Microfilm copy, Southern Historical Collection, University of North Carolina, Chapel Hill.

Bloxham, William D. Letter. Mss. Box 15, P. K. Yonge Library, University of Florida, Gainesville.

Chandler, William Eaton. Papers. Library of Congress, Manuscripts Division.

Clinch, Duncan Lamont. Papers. P. K. Yonge Library.

Cory, J., Jr. Folder. Mss. Box 19, P. K. Yonge Library.

Crummell, Alexander. Papers. Microfilm copy, University of Florida.

Deed Books. Clerk of the Circuit Court, Alachua County Courthouse, Gainesville, Florida.

Deed Books. Clerk of the Circuit Court, Leon County Courthouse, Tallahassee, Florida.

Detwiler, John Y. Narrative. Mss. Box 27, P. K. Yonge Library.

Douglass, Frederick. "Reconstruction." *Atlantic Monthly* 18 (December 1866):761–65.

Gleason, William. Papers. P. K. Yonge Library.

Hart, Ambrose. Letters. P. K. Yonge Library.

Huston, L. D. Papers. Misc. Mss. Box 7, P. K. Yonge Library.

James, Garth. Letters. In possession of William Childers, Gainesville, Florida.

L'Engle, Edward M. Papers. Southern Historical Collection.

Lewis, Charles. Papers. Misc. Mss. Box 15, P. K. Yonge Library.

National Negro Convention, 1835. *Minutes of the Fifth Annual Convention for the Improvement of the Free People of Colour in the United States*. Philadelphia: William P. Gibbons, 1835.

———, 1843. *Minutes of the National Convention of Colored Citizens: Held in Buffalo on the 15th, 16th, 17th, 18th, and 19th of August, 1843, for the Purpose of Considering Their Moral and Political Condition as American Citizens*. New York: Percy and Reed, 1843.

———, 1864. *Proceedings of the National Convention of Colored Men Held in Syracuse, New York, October 4–7, 1864, with the Bill of Wrongs and Rights and Addressed to the American People*. Boston: Printed for the Convention by G. C. Rand and Avery, 1864.

———, 1869. *Proceedings of the Colored National Labor Convention Held in Washington, D.C. on December 6, 7, 8, 9, 10, 1869*. Washington: Office of the *New Era*, 1870.

——, 1869. *Proceedings of the National Convention of the Colored Men of America, Held in Washington, D.C. on January 13, 14, 15, and 16, 1869*. Washington: Great Republic Book and Newspaper Printing Establishment, 1869.
"Proceedings of the Union-Republican Club of Jacksonville." Florida Historical Society Library, University of South Florida, Tampa. Transcript copy, Mss. Box 16, P. K. Yonge Library.
Records of the Board of Public Instruction of Alachua County, Florida.
Report of the Superintendent of Common Schools of Pennsylvania, 1862. Pennsylvania State Library, Harrisburg.
Sanchez, E. C. F. Papers. Misc. Mss. Box 12, P. K. Yonge Library.
Sanford, Henry Shelton. Papers. Box 136, Folder 2, General Sanford Memorial Library, Sanford, Florida. Microfilm copy, P. K. Yonge Library.
Southern States Convention, 1871. *Proceedings of the Southern States Convention of Colored Men Held in Columbia, South Carolina, Commencing October 18, Ending October 25, 1871*. Columbia: Carolina Printing Company, 1871.
Swann, Samuel. Papers. P. K. Yonge Library.
The Watchman's Letter. Mss. Box 1, P. K. Yonge Library.
Webber, Charles Henry "Carl." *The Eden of the South*. New York: n.p., 1883.
Yonge, C. C. Papers. P. K. Yonge Library.
Yulee, David Levy. Papers. P. K. Yonge Library.

NEWSPAPERS

Fernandina Mirror, February 9, July 19, August 30, October 18, 1884.
Fernandina Observer, January 18, 1873.
(Gainesville) *New Era*, February 23, May 4, 18, 25, July 18, November 23, 1867.
Gainesville Sun, September 30, October 16, November 6, 1890.
Gainesville Times, July 6, 1876.
(Gainesville) *Weekly Bee*, May 19, June 9, July 7, 21, August 8, 11, 1882.
(Jacksonville) *Daily Sun and Press*, June 30, 1877.
(Jacksonville) *The Florida Journal*, May 29, June 16, 19, July 3, 10, 14, 17, August 21, 28, 1884.
(Jacksonville) *Florida Sun*, March 11, May 9, 11, 23, 27, June 3, 13, July 1, 1876.
(Jacksonville) *Florida Union*, March 14, 16, May 16, November 9, 1868; February 5, March 12, May 30, June 2, 9, 23, 30, July 7, August 6, 13, September 22, 23, October 8, November 9, 21, 1874; January 31, February 17, March 16, April 20, 26, May 3, 8, June 13, July 18, 27, August 11, 12, 25, September 6, 1876; February 6, September 2, 4, 10, 13, 14, 17, 19, October 5, 8, 9, 11, 1884.
(Jacksonville) *The New South*, July 11, 15, 19, 25, 29, August 12, 15, 26, September 26, 1884.
(Jacksonville) *Tri-Weekly Sun*, January 25, 1876.
(Jacksonville) *Weekly Republican*, February 5, 1873.
Live Oak Times, n.d.
(Martinsburg) *Virginia Free Press*, December 3, 1840.
New Orleans Tribune, July 8, 1865.
New York Herald, May 25, 1871.
New York Times, March 7, 1864; March 2, 1869; December 10–13, 15, 1873; June 1–6, 1884.
New York Tribune, January 24, February 1, 1872.
Palatka Herald, n.d.
(Pensacola) *West Florida Commercial*, December 26, 1867.
(Tallahassee) *Land of Flowers*, July 29, September 20, 1884.
Tallahassee Semi-Weekly Floridian, July 3, 1867.

Tallahassee Sentinel, July 15, 1867; March 19, June 30, 1868; June 11, 15, 25, 30, August 20, 27, September 3, 10, October 1, 8, 22, November 5, 19, December 31, 1870; April 15, May 15, 1871; June 15, August 10, September 21, 28, 1872; May 19, July 18, 1874; July 24, 31, 1875; January 29, June 3, 8, August 5, 19, September 2, 1876.

(Tallahassee) *Weekly Floridian*, July 12, 1867; June 30, July 28, August 11, 1868; August 23, November 22, 1870; October 15, December 5, 12, 19, 1871; October 8, November 5, 1872; January 21, April 22, May 5, September 9, 23, October 7, 28, November 11, 1873; June 2, 23, 30, August 4, September 20, October 28, December 13, 1874; January 8, 1875; August 22, 1876; July 10, 1877; March 5, 1878; January 21, 1879; November 11, December 9, 1884.

Washington Capitol, April 9, 1871.

Washington Daily Morning Chronicle, December 18, July 21, 1869; January 14, October 23, 1871.

(Washington) *Daily National Intelligencer*, February 8, 1866.

(Washington) *New National Era*, January 12, April 6, June 8, July 15, October 26, December 23, 1871; May 2, 1872; October 23, November 4, December 11, 23, 1873.

Washington Star, June 4, 1872.

INTERVIEWS

Jones, Mrs. E. R. Tallahassee, January 15, 1971.
Jones, William. Tallahassee, January 14, 1971.
Means, Miss Etta. Gainesville, April 14, 1971.

FEDERAL DOCUMENTS

"Application for Time Extension. Contested Election of Silas L. Niblack versus Josiah Walls." House of Representatives Archives, National Archives.

Biographical Directory of the American Congress, 1774–1961. Washington: Government Printing Office, 1961.

Congress, United States. 38th Congress, *Congressional Globe*; 42d Congress, *Congressional Globe*, *House Document 22*, *House Miscellaneous Documents 34*, *52*; 43d Congress, *Congressional Globe*, *Congressional Record*, *House Miscellaneous Document 44*, *Senate Report 307*; 44th Congress, *Congressional Record*, *House Miscellaneous Documents 35*, *52*, *Senate Report 611*; 45th Congress, *House Miscellaneous Documents 10*, *52*.

"Company F. Descriptive Book, Third Infantry Regiment, U.S.C.T." National Archives.

Contested Election. Jesse J. Finly [sic] v. Josiah T. Walls. Second Congressional District–Florida. Brief for the Contestee. National Archives.

"J. J. Finley, contestant, and Josiah T. Walls, contestee, 44th Congress: Answer to Notice of contestant." House Archives, Contested Election Files, National Archives.

"Letters and Endorsements, United States Military Records, 1872–1874." National Archives.

Letters Sent from the Assistant Commissioner of Florida. Freedmen's Bureau Records, National Archives.

Naval Academy Records. Register no. 2281. National Archives.

"Orders, Letters, and Roster of Commissioned Officers, Endorsements, and Memoranda, Third Infantry Regiment, U.S.C.T." National Archives.

Paschall, George W. *Contested Election. Silas L. Niblack vs. Josiah T. Walls, from Florida. Argument for Contestant*. Washington: McGill and Witherow, 1872. House Archives, National Archives.

Suits against Defaulting Postmasters, Contractors, and Others, for Debts Due the Post Office Department: *United States vs. Edward L. Young and his Sureties*. Record Group 206, National Archives.

United States Bureau of Refugees, Freedmen, and Abandoned Lands. *Third Semi-Annual Report on Schools for Freedmen, January, 1867*. Washington: Government Printing Office, 1867. Microfilm copy, P. K. Yonge Library.

United States Census, 1870. Microcopy 583, roll 128. P. K. Yonge Library.

Walls, Josiah T. Pension File. *General Index to Pension Files*, 1861–1934, microfilm copy T-288, roll 495. National Archives.

Walls, Josiah T. Service File. *General Index to United States Colored Troops*, microfilm copy 589, roll 90. National Archives.

Ward, William. *List of Cadets Admitted into the United States Military Academy, West Point, N.Y., from Its Origin till September 1, 1886*. Washington: Government Printing Office, 1887. National Archives.

The War of the Rebellion: A Compilation of the Official Records of the Union and Confederate Armies. 70 vols. Washington: Government Printing Office, 1880–1901.

FLORIDA STATE DOCUMENTS

Assembly Journal. A Journal of the Proceedings of the Assembly of the State of Florida, at Its First Session: Begun and Held at the Capitol, in the City of Tallahassee, on Monday, June 8th, 1868. Tallahassee: Office of the *Tallahassee Sentinel*, 1868. Microfilm copy, P. K. Yonge Library.

Assembly Journal. A Journal of the Proceedings of the Assembly of the State of Florida, at an Extra Session Begun and Held at the Capitol, in the City of Tallahassee, on Tuesday, June 8th, 1869. Tallahassee: Edward M. Cheney, 1869. Microfilm copy, P. K. Yonge Library.

Assembly Journal. A Journal of the Proceedings of the Assembly of the State of Florida, at Its Tenth Session, Begun and Held at the Capitol, in the City of Tallahassee, on Tuesday, January 7, 1879. Tallahassee: Charles E. Dyke, 1879.

Florida Executive Department Journal, November 1865 – December 1872. Microfilm copy, P. K. Yonge Library.

Journal of the Proceedings of the Constitutional Convention of the State of Florida Begun and Held at the Capitol, at Tallahassee, on Monday, January 20th, 1868. Tallahassee: Edward M. Cheney, 1868. Microfilm copy, P. K. Yonge Library.

A Journal of the Proceedings of the Joint Convention of the Florida Legislature, Held in the Capitol, November 3, 1868, and of the Senate and Assembly of the State of Florida, at an Extraordinary Session of the Legislature, Convened November 3, 1868. Tallahassee: Office of the *Tallahassee Sentinel*, 1868.

Minutes of the Board of Trustees, Internal Improvement Fund of the State of Florida. Tallahassee: n.p., n.d.

Senate Journal. Journal of the Senate, for the First Session, Fifteenth Legislature, of the State of Florida, Begun and Held at the Capitol, in the City of Tallahassee, on the Eighth Day of June, and Concluded on the Sixth Day of August, in the Year of Our Lord One Thousand Eight Hundred and Sixty Eight. Tallahassee: Office of the *Tallahassee Sentinel*, 1868. Microfilm copy, P. K. Yonge Library.

Senate Journal. A Journal of the Proceedings of the Senate of the State of Florida at the Second Session of the Legislature, Begun and Held at the Capitol in the City of Tallahassee, January 5th, A.D., 1869. Tallahassee: Edward M. Cheney, 1869. Microfilm copy, P. K. Yonge Library.

Senate Journal. A Journal of the Proceedings of the Senate of the State of Florida at the Ninth Session of the Legislature, Begun and Held at the Capitol, in the city of Tallahassee, on Tuesday, January 2, 1877. Tallahassee: Charles E. Dyke, 1877.

Senate Journal. A Journal of the Proceedings of the Senate of the State of Florida, at the Tenth Session of the Legislature, Begun and Held at the Capitol, in the City of Tallahassee, on Tuesday, January 7, 1879. Tallahassee: Charles E. Dyke, 1879.

SECONDARY WORKS

Ackerman, Philip D. "Florida Reconstruction from Walker through Reed, 1865–1873." Master's thesis, University of Florida, 1948.

Aptheker, Herbert, ed. *A Documentary History of the Negro People in the United States*. New York: Citadel Press, 1951.

Barnes, William H. *Our American Government: History of the Forty-Third Congress*. 3 vols. Washington: W. H. Barnes Company, 1875.

Beale, Howard K. *The Critical Year: A Study of Andrew Johnson and Reconstruction*. New York: Frederick Ungar Publishing Company, 1958.

Bell, Howard H. "Expressions of Negro Militancy in the North, 1840–1860." *Journal of Negro History* 45 (January 1960):11–21.

———. "National Negro Conventions of the Middle 1840s: Moral Suasion vs. Political Action." *Journal of Negro History* 42 (October 1957):247–60.

———. "The Negro Emigration Movement, 1849–1854: A Phase of Negro Nationalism." *Phylon* 20 (June 1959):132–44.

———. "A Survey of the Negro Convention Movement, 1830–1861." Ph.D. dissertation, Northwestern University, 1953.

Bentley, George R. *History of the Freedmen's Bureau*. Philadelphia: University of Pennsylvania Press, 1955.

Binder, Frederick M. "Pennsylvania Negro Regiments in the Civil War." *Journal of Negro History* 37 (October 1952):383–417.

Bracey, John H., Meier, August, and Rudwick, Elliott, eds. *Blacks in the Abolitionist Movement*. Belmont, Cal.: Wadsworth Publishing Company, 1971.

Buchholz, F. W. *History of Alachua County, Florida: Narrative and Biographical*. St. Augustine: The Record Company, 1929.

Coulter, E. Merton. *Negro Legislators in Georgia during the Reconstruction Period*. Athens: *Georgia Historical Quarterly*, 1968.

Cox, LaWanda, and Cox, John H. *Politics, Principles and Prejudice, 1865–1866: Dilemma of Reconstruction*. New York: Free Press, 1963.

Davis, T. Frederick. *History of Jacksonville and Vicinity, 1513 to 1924*. Jacksonville: Florida Historical Society, 1925. Facsimile edition, Gainesville: University of Florida Press, 1964.

Davis, William Watson. *The Civil War and Reconstruction in Florida*. New York: Longman's, Green and Company, 1913. Facsimile edition, Gainesville: University of Florida Press, 1964.

Donald, David. *Charles Sumner and the Rights of Man*. New York: Alfred A. Knopf, 1970.

Douglass, Frederick. *Life and Times of Frederick Douglass*. New York: Crowell-Collier Publishing Company, 1962.

———. *Oration by Frederick Douglass Delivered on the Occasion of the Unveiling of the Freedmen's Monument in Memory of Abraham Lincoln in Lincoln Park, Washington, D. C., April 14, 1876*. New York: Frederick Douglass Historical and Cultural League, 1940.

Dyer, Frederick H. *A Compendium of the War of the Rebellion*. 3 vols. New York: T. Yoseloff, 1959.

Foner, Philip S. *The Life and Writings of Frederick Douglass*. New York: International Publishers, 1952.

Fortune, Timothy Thomas. *Black and White: Land, Labor and Politics in the Old South*. New York: Arno Press, 1968.

Franklin, John Hope. *From Slavery to Freedom: A History of the Negro Americans*. 3d ed. New York: Alfred A. Knopf, 1967.

———. *Reconstruction after the Civil War*. Chicago: University of Chicago Press, 1961.

Gardiner, Mabel H., and Gardiner, Ann H. *Chronicles of Old Berkeley: A Narrative History of a Virginia County from its Beginnings to 1926*. Durham: The Seelman Press, 1938.

Gibson, Albert M. *A Political Crime: The History of the Great Fraud*. New York: William S. Gottsberger, 1885.

Grant, Joanne, ed. *Black Protest: History, Documents, and Analyses, 1619 to the Present*. Greenwich, Conn.: Fawcett Publications, 1968.

Green, Constance McLaughlin. *Washington: Village and Capitol, 1800–1878*. Princeton: Princeton University Press, 1962.

Henry, George Selden, Jr. "Radical Republican Policy toward the Negro during Reconstruction, 1862–1872." Ph.D. dissertation, Yale University, 1963.

Henry, Robert Selph. *The Story of Reconstruction*. New York: P. Smith, 1938.

Hildreth, Charles. "A History of Gainesville, Florida." Ph.D. dissertation, University of Florida, 1954.

Hume, Richard L. "The 'Black and Tan' Constitutional Conventions of 1867–1869 in Ten Former Confederate States: A Study of Their Membership." Ph.D. dissertation, University of Washington, 1969.

Johns, John E. *The Civil War in Florida, 1861–1865*. Gainesville: University of Florida Press, 1966.

Klingman, Peter D. "The National Negro Convention Movement, 1864–1872: Black Leadership Attitudes toward the Republican Party." Master's thesis, University of Florida, 1969.

Langley, Lester D. *The Cuban Policy of the United States: A Brief History*. New York: John Wiley and Sons, 1968.

Langston, John Mercer. *Freedom and Citizenship, Selected Lectures*. Washington: n.p., 1883.

Lewis, Elsie M. "The Political Mind of the Negro, 1865–1900." *Journal of Southern History* 21 (May 1955):189–202.

Matison, Sumner Eliot. "The Labor Movement and the Negro during Reconstruction." *Journal of Negro History* 33 (October 1948):426–68.

Mayer, George H. *The Republican Party, 1854–1966*. 2d ed. New York: Oxford University Press, 1967.

McPherson, James M. *The Struggle for Equality: Abolitionists and the Negro in the Civil War and Reconstruction*. Princeton: Princeton University Press, 1964.

Meador, John Allen. "Florida Political Parties, 1865–1877." Ph.D. dissertation, University of Florida, 1964.

Mitchell, C. Bradford. "Paddle-Wheel Inboard: Some of the History of Oklawaha River Steamboating and of the Hart Line." *American Neptune: A Quarterly Journal of Maritime History* 7 (April 1947):115–66.

Morton, Frederick. *The Story of Winchester in Virginia: The Oldest Town in the Shenandoah Valley*. Strasburg, Va.: Shenandoah Publishing House, 1925.

Nevins, Allan, *Hamilton Fish: The Inner History of the Grant Administration*. New York: Dodd, Mead and Company, 1937.

Neyland, Leedell W., and Riley, John W. *The History of Florida Agricultural and Mechanical University*. Gainesville: University of Florida Press, 1963.

Parrish, William E. *Missouri under Radical Rule, 1865–1870*. Columbia: University of Missouri Press, 1965.

Peek, Ralph L. "Aftermath of Military Reconstruction, 1868–1869." *Florida Historical Quarterly* 43 (October 1964):123–41.

———. "Curbing of Voter Intimidation in Florida." *Florida Historical Quarterly* 43 (April 1965):333–48.

———. "Election of 1870 and the End of Reconstruction in Florida." *Florida Historical Quarterly* 45 (April 1967):352–68.

———. "Lawlessness and the Restoration of Order in Florida, 1868–1871." Ph.D. dissertation, University of Florida, 1964.

Rhodes, James Ford. *History of the United States from the Compromise of 1850.* 8 vols. New York: Macmillan Company, 1892–1906.

Richardson, James D. *A Compilation of the Messages and Papers of the Presidents, 1789–1902.* 20 vols. Washington: Bureau of National Literature and Art, 1896–1907.

Richardson, Joe M. *The Negro in the Reconstruction of Florida, 1865–1877.* Tallahassee: Florida State University Press, 1965.

Rollin, Frank A. *Life and Public Services of Martin R. Delany.* Boston: Lee and Shepard, 1883.

Shofner, Jerrell H. "The Constitution of 1868." *Florida Historical Quarterly* 41 (April 1963):356–74.

————. "Fraud and Intimidation in the Florida Election of 1876." *Florida Historical Quarterly* 42 (April 1964):321–30.

————. "The Labor League of Jacksonville: A Negro Union and White Strikebreakers." *Florida Historical Quarterly* 50 (January 1972):278–82.

————. "Political Reconstruction in Florida." *Florida Historical Quarterly* 45 (October 1966):145–70.

Simkins, Francis B. "New Viewpoints of Southern Reconstruction." *Journal of Southern History* 5 (February 1939):49–61.

Smith, Samuel Denny. *The Negro in Congress, 1870–1901.* Chapel Hill: University of North Carolina Press, 1940.

Swint, Henry. *The Northern Teacher in the South, 1862–1870.* New York: Octagon Books, 1967.

Tocqueville, Alexis de. *Democracy in America.* 2 vols. New York: Alfred A. Knopf, 1945.

Trelease, Allen W. *White Terror: The Ku Klux Conspiracy and Southern Reconstruction.* New York: Harper and Row, 1971.

Wallace, John. *Carpetbag Rule in Florida.* Jacksonville: Da Costa Printing and Publishing House, 1888. Facsimile edition, Gainesville: University of Florida Press, 1964.

Wesley, Charles H. *Negro Labor in the United States.* New York: Vanguard Press, 1927.

Williamson, Edward C. "Independentism: A Challenge to the Florida Democracy of 1884." *Florida Historical Quarterly* 27 (October 1948):131–56.

Wood, Forrest G. "On Revising Reconstruction History: Negro Suffrage, White Disfranchisement, and Common Sense." *Journal of Negro History* 51 (April 1966):98–113.

Woodward, C. Vann. *Reunion and Reaction.* Boston: Little, Brown, and Company, 1951.

Index

153